D1443342

●●●●●●●●●●●●●●●●●●●●●●●●●●●●●●●●●●●●●●

Legal Liability in Psychotherapy

*A Practitioner's
Guide to
Risk Management*

Benjamin M. Schutz

Legal Liability
in Psychotherapy

Jossey-Bass Publishers
San Francisco • Washington • London • 1982

LEGAL LIABILITY IN PSYCHOTHERAPY
A Practitioner's Guide to Risk Management
by Benjamin M. Schutz

Copyright © 1982 by: Jossey-Bass Inc., Publishers
433 California Street
San Francisco, California 94104
&
Jossey-Bass Limited
28 Banner Street
London EC1Y 8QE

Library of Congress Cataloging in Publication Data

Schutz, Benjamin M.
    Legal liability in psychotherapy.

    Bibliography: p. 185
    Includes index.
    1. Psychotherapists—Malpractice—United
States. I. Title.
KF2910.P753S35   346.7303'32   81-19321
ISBN 0-87589-512-3   347.306332   AACR2

Manufactured in the United States of America

JACKET DESIGN BY WILLI BAUM

FIRST EDITION

Code 8202

●●●●●●●●●●●●●●●●●●●●●●●●●●●●●●●●●●●●●●

The Jossey-Bass
Social and Behavioral Science Series

Preface

Zigmond Lebensohn (1978) recently wrote a paper titled "Defensive Psychiatry or How to Treat the Mentally Ill Without Being a Lawyer." His answer to that question is "very carefully." The purpose of this book is to give substance to the term "very carefully." Specifically, it attempts to explain the law's view of our roles as therapists; to discuss the various types of liability available to plaintiffs seeking recompense; and to give therapists concrete suggestions for avoiding risk in the known high-risk areas, without the loss of clinical efficiency.

Whenever I talk about legal liability for psychotherapy, I am struck by the intense anxiety and anger that the topic evokes. These feelings seem to arise because, in general, we therapists feel uncomfortable about being scrutinized and held legally accountable for our practices. Many of us do not seem confident about what we are doing or how it looks to others. From my talks with therapists, a picture has emerged of our collective view of the law. It is seen as an unreasonable and capricious parent, inventing full-blown duties and then holding us accountable retroactively (most notably, in the *Tarasoff* case); as a frustrating discipline that functions far better as an adversary than an adviser, rarely able to provide guidelines for avoiding problems; as a nit-picking nuisance concerned with form and not substance, where the complex realities of human interaction are whittled away in semantics; and, finally, as a parent who does not understand or appreciate the difficulty of the task we have undertaken and who holds us accountable to patently unfair standards.

Some therapists react to all this by avoiding the issue altogether. They cite the relatively low incidence of suits and the fact that the suits people hear about often involve outrageously unprofessional conduct. It is, of course, easy to point to flagrant misconduct and say, "That's not me," and let the issue drop. The painful reality is that one may be functioning as an ethical and competent therapist on a case and still face a lawsuit; that is, ethical and competent behavior is not an absolute bar to a legitimate suit. Malpractice is the dark side of the American dream—a true democracy, for anyone can grow up to be a precedent.

Other therapists, instead of avoiding the issue, react with passive-aggressive hypercompliance. They out-legalize the lawyers and avoid pushing at their own or their patients' frontiers. For example, they avoid discussions of violent impulses and seek to resolve all human difficulties in paperwork. Their adherence to the law does undermine clinical effectiveness—exactly what the angry therapists contend.

What I am suggesting to therapists is exactly the situation that we present our patients—that risk is inevitable in all worthwhile ventures. There are no guarantees. We cannot, and should not, fail to undertake a project because of the risk, or be more concerned with safety than with healing. Instead, we need to get all the information we can to guide our decisions, no matter how unpalatable. We can then make our risks the irreducible ones; or, at least, we can make our decisions with full knowledge of the cost-benefit ratio.

After reviewing thousands of pages of legal commentary, I have concluded that the law does not fully appreciate the complexity or the demands of our tasks. However, ours is one of the few professions allowed by law to provide in-house, expert testimony in a court to explain our behavior and its outcomes. My biggest complaint with the law is that, on the one hand, it encourages patient equality and, on the other hand, it holds professionals accountable for the behavior of their patients. Nonetheless, I hope in this book to offer guidelines on how to cope with the law as it is, not to turn our backs on it because it is not as we would like it. I do not want to discourage efforts to bring the law into a more sophisticated appreciation of therapeutic rights, duties, process, and outcomes. However, that task is not within my scope here.

This book addresses the documented high-risk clinical decision-making areas encountered by therapists, regardless of their formal training, theoretical orientation, or treatment setting. It is intended to be useful to the psychiatrist, psychologist, social worker, or psychiatric nurse in private or public practice, whether from a behavior modification, Gestalt, psychodynamic, or other approach. Whenever these factors (formal training, theoretical orientation, and treatment setting) significantly affect the degree or type of risk, they will be addressed. Otherwise, the generic term *therapist* or *psychotherapist* will be used to identify the practitioner. Psychotherapy is meant to include all activities directly and primarily aimed at altering behavior or internal thinking and feeling states of a person, as executed by a person (therapist) entrusted by either the individual in question or society to have the expertise to do so. Interventions may occur at different levels, on a continuum from the physical to the symbolic. The phrase "directly and primarily" is used to distinguish psychotherapy from other activities, such as case management, linking (liasons between agencies or practitioners), and advocacy (of patients' rights in a helping system), where the behavioral/mentation changes are derivative effects, not primary ones.

The chapters are organized around risk areas most frequently cited in suits. However, since court reports of decisions are almost never published below the appellate level, these areas possibly represent only the tip of the iceberg. We have no access to records of cases decided at trial level and never appealed or to cases settled out of court. There may be other areas of even greater risk, which we, as a profession, are unaware of because of the disparity between incidence and reporting.

Chapter One discusses the types of legal liability that can be applied to the therapeutic process: torts, unintentional (that is, suits charging professional negligence or malpractice) and intentional; contract law; constitutional and criminal law; and

product liability law. The major concepts relevant to each type
of liability are introduced. (They are referred to again in later
chapters as they are made manifest in particular high-risk situations.) Issues of immunity and insurance coverage are also discussed.

Chapter Two deals with high-risk areas in the establishment of the therapeutic framework—especially, informed consent (based on information that must be disclosed to the patient
—particularly, information concerning the diagnosis and innovative therapies, if such are to be attempted) and implicit and explicit contracts. Chapter Three moves on to high-risk areas in
the management of the therapeutic process. Included are issues
of undue influence, consultation and supervisory liability, termination and abandonment, and record keeping.

Chapters Four and Five address the problems of the high-
risk patient: the homicidal and the suicidal patient. These chapters focus on the problems of the foreseeability of risk and the
clinical management of the high-risk patient. There is an extensive discussion of the *Tarasoff* case and subsequent ones concerning the "duty to warn."

Chapter Six covers high-risk areas in the somatic therapies—specifically, therapy involving drugs and electroconvulsive therapy. Issues of informed consent, patient management
on drugs and electroconvulsive therapy, and the particular problems that the tardive dyskinesia syndrome raise are discussed.

In Chapter Seven suggestions are made for the professions
involved in the practice of psychotherapy to respond to the current malpractice boom in this country in ways that will bring
about better care for all patients.

The book closes with a selection of resources: codes of
professional ethics and standards of practice. These resources
are included to provide guidelines and to stimulate thought
about what our professions deem the "standard of care." As
Chapter One indicates, the law will hold us to a "standard of
care" in determining negligence.

Nothing in this book guarantees to prevent a suit, which
initially exists only in the mind of the aggrieved, or guarantees
victory in a courtroom. The book does represent an exhaustive
researching of extant cases and legal and mental health com-

mentary designed to produce reasonable and prudent considerations for risk management. All suggestions should be reviewed by an attorney first, for their compliance with existing laws. They represent possible responses to known high-risk areas, and their implementation should be integrated in each case with the practitioner's clinical expertise and knowledge about the needs of each patient. I hope that they will stimulate further thought about these issues in each therapist's daily practice and will not be applied in a rote manner as "the answer to the problem." I am not an attorney, and this book should not be read as if it were legal advice. In fact, my first suggestion is that—before they find themselves waist deep in alligators—therapists should cultivate a good relationship with an attorney well versed in mental health liability issues.

I thank the following people for their indispensable help in bringing this project to fruition: First, my wife, JoAnne Lindenberger, saw this project as necessary to my own vitality and endorsed and protected the solitude necessary to do the research and writing. My brother, Adam Schutz, tirelessly tracked down and copied references for me at the Library of Congress, sparing me the burden of that joyless job. Neil Ruther read the manuscript from a lawyer's perspective, to make sure that my understanding of legal concepts and doctrines was accurate. Joseph R. Sanders read the manuscript as an experienced clinician and also—in his role as the American Psychological Association's administrative officer for ethics—as one well versed in current legal and ethical dilemmas for psychotherapists. He helped shape the manuscript into a book useful for the practicing therapist. Both of my readers were productively critical and prompt in reviewing the manuscript, and their suggestions helped make this a better book. My typist, Constance Robinson, swiftly and amazingly converted my road-map drafts into workable manuscripts. And my friend Steven Spruill, who has been an enthusiastic believer in my ability to write, offered unstintingly of his experience as a novelist.

Falls Church, Virginia   Benjamin M. Schutz
November 1981

Contents

The Author

Benjamin M. Schutz is a clinical psychologist engaged in the private practice of psychotherapy in Springfield, Virginia. He received his B.A. degree in psychology from Lafayette College (1971) and his Ph.D. in clinical psychology from the Catholic University of America (1977).

He is a certified psychologist in Maryland, a licensed psychologist in Washington, D.C., and a licensed clinical psychologist in Virginia; and he holds a certificate from the Council for the National Register of Health Service Providers in Psychology. A member of the Divisions of Psychotherapy and Psychoanalysis of the American Psychological Association, the American Society of Psychologists in Private Practice, and the Northern Virginia Society of Clinical Psychologists, he is currently pursuing a Diplomate from the American Board of Forensic Psychology. Prior to entering private practice, he was the coordinator of Services for Abused Children and Their Families at the Mt. Vernon Center for Community Mental Health, Alexandria, Virginia, and the Mental Health Services member of the Fairfax County Multidiscipline Child Protection Team. He is currently at work on a book about psychotherapy as applied moral philosophy.

●●●●●●●●●●●●●●●●●●●●●●●●●●●●●●●●●●●●●

Legal Liability in Psychotherapy

*A Practitioner's
Guide to
Risk Management*

1

●●●●●●●●●●●●●●●●●●●●●●●●●●●●●●●●●●●●●

Legal Liability Affecting Psychotherapists

●●●●●●●●●●●●●●●●●●●●●●●●●●●●●●●●●●●●●

The vast majority of suits against therapists, including malpractice, have been founded in tort law, although suits founded in contract law have been increasing in recent years. Only rarely has liability been sought on criminal grounds or for violations of constitutional law. Thus, the major areas of risk for therapists are those centered on civil liability, including malpractice, intentional torts, and contract law.

Torts and contracts are part of civil law. They are derived from statutes, constitutional and common law, or case law precedents. They differ from criminal law in that they pertain to acts offensive to an individual, not to society in general. An offensive act may be tried civilly (when an individual brings suit to recover damages) or as a criminal offense (when the state brings suit to protect society). Neither action excludes the possibility of the other. In fact, proponents in the growing victims' rights movement have initiated civil suits against criminals whose sentences are felt to be too light.

In general, a tort is a type of harm done to an individual

1

in such a manner that the law orders the person who does the harm to pay damages to the injured party. Torts may be intentional or unintentional. Of the unintentional torts, negligence is our chief concern. Negligence pertains to the standard of care a reasonable person takes in his relationship with his fellow men so as not to unduly increase the risk of harm to them. When a professional acts negligently toward a person within the parameters of the professional relationship, his action constitutes malpractice. When applied to a psychotherapist in the treatment of a patient, malpractice may be defined as an act or omission that falls below the standard of reasonable care and skill and that results in or aggravates an injury to the patient. The standard of reasonable care is the care and skill usually exercised by psychotherapists in good standing of the same school or system of practice in the nation.

Many of the acts that would form the basis for a malpractice suit can also be brought up as tortious actions in themselves (that is, as intentional torts), without the plaintiff's having to show negligent professional care. For example, a breach of confidentiality may be pursued as malpractice or as the tort of defamation of character. For reasons that I will give later, pursuit of these acts as intentional torts (apart from negligence) is more likely to be successful for the patient than a negligence action, yet malpractice suits are far more common—apparently because insurance for malpractice makes therapists attractive targets for a negligence action, in the eyes of both plaintiffs and attorneys. In general, intentional torts are easier for therapists to avoid but harder to defeat in court; by its vagueness, malpractice is harder to avoid but easier to defeat in court.

Unintentional Torts: Malpractice

The definition of malpractice contains four key elements necessary to prove the tort: (1) that a therapist-patient relationship was established; (2) that the therapist's conduct fell below the acceptable standard of care; (3) that this conduct was the proximate cause of an injury to the patient; (4) that an actual injury was sustained by the patient.

Professional Relationship. The existence of the patient-therapist relationship is generally the easiest of the four elements to prove; usually, a bill for the therapist's services is sufficient evidence. Whether a professional relationship exists between a patient and a court-ordered psychiatric or psychological examiner is a disputed area. In this situation, the examiner is usually seen as a quasi-judicial figure whose primary duty is to the court.

Standard of Care. For several reasons, establishing the standard of care for a case is difficult. First, there are numerous schools that advocate different treatment approaches to the same presenting problem. As professionals practicing therapy, we have been given the privilege of largely setting the legal standards of conduct by in-house expert testimony. The privilege is not absolute. In some cases, the court has determined that the standards of a profession were not adequate safeguards for the public and that compliance with accepted standards was *persuasive but not conclusive* evidence against negligence. For instance, in *Helling* v. *Carey,* 519 P.2d 981 (Wash. 1974), the court cited Justice Learned Hand in the *T. J. Hooper* case (60 F.2d 737 (2d Cir. 1932)): "A whole calling may have unduly lagged in the adoption of new and available devices. It never may set its own tests, however persuasive be its usages. Courts must in the end say what is required; there are precautions so imperative that even their universal disregard will not excuse their omission." Hence, a therapist can be regarded as competent by his profession and still be found liable. However, the likelihood of such an unfortunate precedent is small. The courts have been chary about setting standards in our field. With the variety of schools in existence, almost any treatment activity probably is endorsed somewhere. According to Prosser (1964), the expert on torts, "Where there are different schools of medical thought . . . the doctor is entitled to be judged according to the tenets of the school he professes to follow" (p. 163). A school of thought "must be a recognized one with definite principles, and it must be the line of thought of at least a respectable minority of the profession" (p. 165). However, a plaintiff's attorney may argue that the entire school is wrong! A parade of experts, each contradicting the other, will not inspire confidence in jurors; and a school that does not have a clear, commonsense base may be utterly demolished by an experienced trial attorney.

There are two situations where one might *not* be judged according to the tenets of a particular school. (1) If the therapist does not profess membership (for example, if he describes his work as eclectic), he will then be held to the standard of care of a therapist in good standing, who will act as expert witness in his case. (2) If his approach is so innovative that he is the only person capable of expert testimony, his testimony will be held to a general standard of reasonableness, as evaluated by the judge and/or jury.* Obviously, if one adheres to a particular school, the scope of a standard of care is clarified. Such clarity helps the therapist if he falls within the scope, but it may hurt him if his practices are at odds with the school's principles or with commonsense expectations; innovation *could* appear as negligence.

If a therapist presents himself as a specialist, he will be held to the highest standards of a specialist, even if that claim is a misrepresentation. Again, the standard of care is determined by expert witnesses of the defendant's school, who testify to accepted practice on a national level. The "locality rule," holding one only to the standard of practitioners in one's community, used to operate; with knowledge increasingly accessible, however, the "locality rule" has been replaced by national standards of practice. In addition to expert testimony, published professional standards are allowed as a yardstick in a minority of states, particularly if they are the standards of a school or group with which the defendant identifies.

One significant doctrine that may obviate the need for expert testimony and that, in fact, shifts the burden of proof onto the defendant-therapist, is *res ipsa loquitur* ("the act

---

*The traditional use of the pronoun *he* has not yet been superseded by a convenient, generally accepted pronoun that means either *he* or *she*. Therefore, the author will continue to use *he* while acknowledging the inherent inequity of the traditional preference of the masculine pronoun.

speaks for itself"). Essentially, the plaintiff introduces this doctrine in cases where the negligence is felt to be so self-evident that any reasonable common man—in this case the judge and jury members—can see it. Then it becomes the therapist's responsibility to show that the act is not negligence. Technically, three criteria (Wigmore, 1961) must be met for this doctrine to be accepted in court: (1) The injury sustained does not ordinarily occur in the absence of negligence. (2) The injury must have been caused by elements within the exclusive control of the defendant. (3) The injury must not have been due to any voluntary action or contribution on the plaintiff's part. The third criterion may be disposed of in states that recognize the concept of comparative negligence, which allows for liability to be apportioned according to the percentage contributed by the plaintiff and the defendant. Contributory negligence—that is, any contribution whatsoever by the plaintiff—is generally held to be a bar to the use of the *res ipsa loquitur* doctrine.

A second doctrine, that of negligence per se, may also obviate the need for expert testimony. Negligence per se is the judicial rule that a violation of statute, governmental guidelines (such as the National Institute of Mental Health standards), or a court order *may* be a basis for action when (1) the injured party is a member of the class for whose benefit the statute was enacted, (2) the resultant injury is of the type contemplated by the statute, and (3) the breach is the proximate cause of the injury. The reasoning behind this rule is that statutes are formulated to be the standard of reasonable conduct and embody the experience of the entire community, which may have had the benefit of expert testimony in hearings to draft the guidelines or statutes. In order to avoid an unintentional violation, the therapist doing "court-ordered" treatment should obtain a copy of the actual *written* order, not the probation officer's interpretation of the meaning of the order, before beginning treatment.

In general, to show breach of a standard of care once the standard has been determined, the plaintiff must show that the therapist did not exercise (1) the minimally accepted degree of knowledge or skill possessed by other practitioners or (2) the minimally acceptable degree of care, attention, diligence, or vigilance exercised in the application of those skills.

Proximate Cause. Once the plaintiff demonstrates that a breach of standard of care has occurred, he must then show that the breach was the legal or proximate cause of the injury. Proximate cause may be defined as a cause that produces the injury in a natural and continuous sequence, unbroken by any independent intervening causes. In other words, the breach must be the sole cause of the injury; no other intervening causes can be accepted. If the initial breach creates a situation in which another reasonably foreseeable cause is introduced—that is, if the intervening cause occurred *only* because of the initial breach—the chain is also considered unbroken.

Proximate cause is becoming easier to establish with the advent of the newer, more directive therapies. In the past, to trace an analyst's nods, uh-huhs, or interpretations as causal agents to an actual injury was almost impossible. Today, however, therapists who give directives for concrete action make it far easier for a court to perceive the links between the therapist's actions and injury. For example, a therapist, in an attempt to reestablish proper hierarchies of authority in a family, may direct a father to forcibly carry a recalcitrant adolescent to his room whenever he misbehaves. This therapist may find himself facing a lawsuit if Junior clobbers the old man or is dropped and falls down the stairs, or if Father has a heart attack from the stress. Dawidoff (1973a), a legal scholar in this area, recommends that therapists limit themselves to *suggestions* for action, not *prescriptions* for action. This approach makes the causal link weaker by interposing the patient and his decision to try out the suggestion as the proximate cause. However, it undercuts the therapist's potency when he does make a directive. At least in part, the appearance of preemptory authority is what makes the family follow through with difficult courses of action. The therapist, being the one who commands the action, will then draw the fire of the offended parties, thereby preserving some of the positive ties between family members. Making only suggestions may be safer, but it probably decreases some of the therapist's potency as a change agent. Moreover, the therapist could still be held liable if the patient was of such a make-up—for example, a passive-dependent personality—as to be unable to appreciate the distinction between suggestions and prescriptions. The argument would be that the therapist, by virtue of his special knowledge, should have known that the patient was the sort who would unreflectively do anything that the therapist mentioned.

Considering what Dawidoff suggests about prescribing action, paradoxical forms of intervention, such as prescribing the symptom, will appear quite puzzling to a judge or jury. Should an injury occur, the therapist would have to utilize expert testimony to try to show that the course of action was reasonable and hence avoid a *res ipsa loquitur* motion that, on the face of it, an act—for example, the therapist's suggestion that his insomniac patient stay awake all night—was negligent. Paradoxical interventions are precisely the kinds of action that an attorney will focus on in an attempt to discredit the entire school of thought. Behaviorally oriented therapists are also easier to assail because their procedures are specified and directly relate to overt patient behavior. Also, these schools openly espouse a position of power and responsibility for producing change. Thus, the outcome, positive or negative, is seen to be the result of therapist factors—not patient factors, such as resistance to treatment.

A major defense against findings of negligence is the concept of contributory negligence on the patient's part as an intervening cause breaking the chain of causality between a therapist's acts and the injury. This doctrine is not applicable to children or to patients whom a judge has declared mentally incompetent (as a result of physical and/or mental illness). What must be proven is that the patient's acts fell below the level of self-care that the average person would have exercised under the same or similar circumstances. The point arises whether mental illness is a defense against a charge of contributory negligence. This point is detailed in Chapter Five on the suicidal patient, for it is there, when the patient dies by his own hand, that the concept is most often used. In such instances, a plaintiff will argue that, as a profoundly depressed person, the patient could not have been expected to act reasonably and therefore could not be charged with contributory negligence.

Proximate cause is easier to prove if the acts in question and the injury are closely related in time. Hence, as the time draws on from act to injury, the chance for intervening variables to intercede increases. States arbitrarily set statutes of limitations on negligence cases, thereby setting a limit on liability. It is important to know the statute of limitation in one's own jurisdiction and whether it is dated from the day of the actual injury or of the *discovery* of the injury. It should also be noted that a minor's right to sue begins when he comes of age, so one may be sued by a child's parents as friends of the child *res judicata* (in matters to be determined by a court) or, up to eighteen years later, be sued by the child, now an adult. Thus, the effective statute of limitations as applied to the treatment of minors is eighteen years plus the state's statute. The tolling of the statute of limitations is delayed by the duration of a continuing course of action. A continuing course of action may be repeated acts of negligence. Thus, the statute of limitations begins when the negligence ends, not when it began. A continuing course of action also may be a patient's incompetence. His right to sue begins when he is competent to do so, even if that is forty years after the original injury.

Injury. If proximate cause is shown, an injury must have resulted from it. There are numerous injuries that can be claimed. Strupp, Hadley, and Gomes-Schwartz (1977) offer a partial list of negative effects:

1. Exacerbation of the presenting symptoms (including decompensation or regression, increased depression, inhibitions, extension of phobias, increased somatic difficulties, decreased self-esteem, paranoia, obsessional symptoms, guilt, decrease in impulse control).
2. Appearance of new symptoms (including psychotic break or dissociations, severe psychosomatic reactions, suicide attempt, development of new forms of acting out, disruption of previously solid relationships).
3. Patient misuse or abuse of therapy (generally settling into a

dependent relationship that is more gratifying than the "real" world, increase in intellectualization to avoid action or as a mere change of obsessional thoughts, therapy as a place to merely ventilate hostile feelings and have them rationalized, increased reliance on irrationality and "spontaneity" to avoid reflection on real-world limits).

4. Patients overextending themselves in taking on tasks before they can adequately achieve them, possibly to please the therapist or due to inappropriate directives, leading to failure, guilt, or self-contempt.

5. Disillusionment with therapy, leading to feelings of hopelessness in getting help from any relationship.

Other negative effects often cited by plaintiffs as iatrogenic injuries include damages due to reliance on a therapist's directives, leading to divorce, job loss, economic loss, emotional harm, injury to reputation, loss of companionship, incarceration, suicide or death of third party, self- or non-self-inflicted injuries, deprivation of constitutional rights, and/or loss of liberty or privacy.

Damages. If these four elements are proven, then damages will be awarded to the plaintiff. The standard of proof in a civil case is the preponderance of the evidence (numerically, this may be conceived of as a 51-49 split of the evidence), a lower standard than the criminal one of reasonable doubt. Damages can be of two types—compensatory for the injury or punitive as a punishment for wanton, reckless, or heinous acts. Compensatory damages generally address the following areas: (1) past earnings lost, (2) future earnings lost, (3) pain and suffering, (4) restitution to undo the damage, (5) the cost of the therapy itself.

There are substantial difficulties for a plaintiff to prove the four elements of a malpractice action. These difficulties center on the two elements of standard of care and proximate cause. First of all, because of the absence of witnesses, it may be impossible to prove what things were said or done in an individual therapy session. Second, barring gross misconduct, the enormous range of options in treatment allows for great latitude in acceptable care. Third, since the "natural" course of "mental illness" is unknown, it is difficult to prove that the therapist's action or inaction proximately caused the harm. The injury *might* have been the "natural" result of the illness. The ebb and flow of therapy—the plateaus, impasses, and regressions prior to new reorganizations—make it very difficult to establish a pre-injury baseline of emotional functioning in psychotherapy.

Intentional Torts

The vagueness of the elements of proof in negligence invites more suits than for other tort actions but, at the same time, makes them harder for the plaintiffs to win. In contrast, the relative clarity of the elements of proof for other tort actions makes them easier to prevent but harder to defeat in court. Generally, expert testimony is not needed for intentional torts. The major tort actions filed are the following:

Assault and Battery. Assault means that, without consent, the patient was placed in reasonable apprehension of immediate harmful or offensive touching and the defendant-therapist had the apparent ability to inflict harmful or offensive touching. Battery means that, without consent, the therapist did perform some harmful or offensive touching. Harmful is defined as being productive of pain, injury, or bodily impairment; and offensive refers to a reasonable person's sense of dignity. Only three elements need be proven in this tort: lack of informed consent, proximate cause, and injury. What is missing here is the question of a standard of care. The quality of the performance is not the question. The consent is. For example, successful Rolfing that was not adequately consented to, and in the process was found offensive or painful, could be subject to a tort action as assault and battery.

Defamation of Character. Defamation of character may be oral, as in slander, or written, as in libel. It must be published (made public), and it must be injurious to the reputation of the plaintiff. There are three avenues of defense to this tort: (1) An absolute bar to liability is that the revelation is true. (2) An informed consent to release the information would indicate that the plaintiff had no reason to bar the publication. (3) The defendant can invoke the doctrine of "qualified privilege," or overarching social duty to release the information. *Berry* v. *Moensch,* 8 Utah 2d 191, 331 P.2d 814 (1958), elaborated on this doctrine, setting forth the following four conditions: (1) The information must be presented in good faith, not in malice. (2) There must be a legitimate social duty to release the information. (3) The disclosure must be limited in scope to what is necessary to discharge the duty. (4) The disclosure must be only to the appropriate parties with a right to know.

Invasion of Privacy. Invasion of privacy is a violation of the right to be left alone. It requires that private facts be disclosed to more than a small group of persons, and such disclosure must be offensive to a reasonable person of ordinary sensibilities. The avenue of liability in this tort is strict liability; that is, the fact of the intrusion itself is the cause of action, regardless of the intent or negligence. Invasion of privacy can be distinguished from defamation of character on two grounds: (1) even complimentary material can be an invasion of privacy; (2) the intrusion into privacy does not require publication of private information—merely the intrusion into the person's private spheres. This tort requires extremely unreasonable or offensive conduct. A therapist who makes phone calls to a patient's place of work, identifying himself as a therapist, or who sends bills and correspondence to a patient, with an identification of his relationship to the patient, might give grounds for an invasion of privacy action. The presence of nonessential staff in treatment settings has been viewed as an intrusion on the patient's seclusion. The patient has an absolute right to refuse to be interviewed as a "case conference." The certain defense to this tort is consent.

Malicious Prosecution and False Imprisonment. The tort of malicious prosecution is very difficult to prove, since it hinges on proving malicious intent on the part of the defendant, and even grossly destructive behavior can occur without the requisite malice. To prove false imprisonment—a charge often made when there has been an involuntary commitment—a plaintiff must establish the absence of probable cause or the failure to adhere to due process. The injury in both of these torts is usually deprivation of liberty.

Infliction of Emotional Duress. The tort of infliction of emotional duress usually requires outrageous conduct on the defendant's part. The harm done is the infliction of emotional pain, distress, or suffering. As such, this tort may be attached to any of a number of other actions.

Abuse of Process. Abuse of process refers to the use of legal process against another to accomplish a purpose for which the legal action was not designed. This charge is most often made about involuntary commitment hearings, where the plaintiff believes that the real intent of the proceeding was merely to detain him, not to determine his need for treatment.

Fraudulent Misrepresentation. Fraud is the intentional or negligent, implied or direct, perversion of truth for the purpose of inducing another, who relies on such misrepresentation, to part with something valuable belonging to him or to surrender a legal right. If one misrepresents the risks or benefits of therapy for one's own benefit and not the patient's, so as to induce him to undergo treatment and pay the fee, this is fraud. Telling a patient that sexual intercourse is therapy may be seen as a perversion of the truth so as to get the patient to part with something of value. Hence, this would be seen as fraud.

Contract Law

A relatively infrequent approach to legal liability for psychotherapy is through contract law. The law is quite ambiguous about the way it views the nature of the psychotherapeutic relationship. On the one hand, many of the duties derived seem to come from a conception of the therapist-patient relationship as a fiduciary one. Basically, a fiduciary relationship is one based on trust; and the therapist, as the fiduciary of the patient's trust, cannot serve his own needs in preference to those of the patient. (A therapist is not strictly a fiduciary because the requirement of absolute candor is not present. The therapeutic privilege—instances where the therapist withholds information

in the interest of the patient and the treatment—may contra-
indicate it; and the maintenance of early rapport, so that later
confrontations may be handled, also cuts into the degree of candor that best serves the patient.) On the other hand, since the
therapeutic relationship is also a fee-for-services relationship,
there are implied contractual elements to the relationship. The
fee-for-services aspect of the relationship means that the therapist may have a compelling personal interest to balance with
his clients' interests; namely, preserving his income. He may
therefore be open to a charge of fiduciary abuse when he recommends that a patient not terminate therapy or that a patient
increase the frequency of his sessions.

How do these two sets of expectancies stand in relation
to each other? Can a therapist contract with a patient not to
provide certain usually accepted fiduciary duties, such as responding to after-hours emergency calls or sharply curtailing the
scope of confidentiality? One legal commentator (Tarshis, 1972)
has written that the legal duties of the therapist arise from the
relationship, not from contract, and cannot be limited only to
those agreed on or bargained for by contract. What is certain is
that both approaches can be used as avenues of liability. The
use of explicit contracts for treatment can protect the therapist
by clarifying roles and duties. The therapist can shape such a
contract to reflect accurately what he feels he can provide for a
fee. At the same time, precisely because of their clarity, ex-
pressed contracts can make breach of contract or warranty easier to prove. Moreover, reducing the complex relationship of
psychotherapy to the small portion of the interaction covered
in an explicit contract may reinforce the patient's tendency to
view the relationship solely in terms of the behavior described
in the contract, thus increasing the likelihood of litigation
(though not necessarily the success rate), because the patient
may feel that he can clearly point to the contract and say "I
didn't get what I paid for."

If the therapist tells a patient that the treatment will be
successful, he can be sued for a breach of warranty if the outcome he predicts does not occur. Reassurances should be
couched in probabilistic terms. If a therapist holds himself out

as a guarantor of success, he will be held to that, even though it is not a duty normally imposed.

Constitutional Law

Recent landmark cases (*Wyatt* v. *Stickney*, 325 F. Supp. 781 (Ala. 1971), 344 F. Supp. 373 (M.D. Ala. 1972), *Wyatt* v. *Aderholt*, 503 F.2d 1305 (5th Cir. 1974)) have applied constitutional law to the provision of mental health services. These cases were class action suits filed on behalf of involuntarily committed patients at Bryce Hospital in Tuscaloosa, Alabama, against officials in the Alabama state government. The suits alleged that the operation of the state facilities was such that it precluded any therapeutic benefits for those committed to the facilities. The courts found against the state of Alabama and took a substantial step toward articulating what the "right to treatment" means in everyday treatment of involuntarily committed patients.

The violation of the rights guaranteed by the Constitution may be a source of action in itself, or it may be cited as injuries in a tort action (for example, loss of the right to liberty in a negligent commitment action). These actions are most often pursued on behalf of involuntarily committed patients but are not limited to that population.

Constitutional law can be invoked only if the therapist's actions were pursued under "color of state law." A conservative interpretation of this difficult concept is that, for an individual's actions to be a constitutional violation, the individual must be acting in the state's interest. In a most liberal interpretation, any therapist licensed by a state is acting under the color of state law.

The following actions have been pursued in regard to specific therapeutic approaches: (1) the right to due process in commitment situations; (2) the right to be free of cruel or unusual punishment in aversive therapy treatments; (3) the right to be free from involuntary servitude in token economies; (4) the right to privacy; (5) the right to treatment and the right to refuse treatment. The last two rights (the right to treatment and the right to refuse treatment) have led to much gnashing of teeth by mental health professionals. The right to treatment means that mere custodial care or a nebulous milieu therapy is not sufficient. That is, as established in *Wyatt* v. *Stickney,* a patient has a right to an individualized treatment program, to be implemented in the least restrictive environment, with clear statements of problems and goals; a rationale for the methods used to achieve the goals, along with a proposed timetable; specification of therapist responsibilities; and criteria for release or discharge. These standards, while not directly mandated for voluntary patients, can be met through the use of a treatment contract. It is unclear whether a patient in a voluntary program has the right to have the program tailored to his needs, and not be assigned to a program he fits. Clearly, for an involuntary patient, the program must be fitted to the patient, not the patient to the program.

The right to refuse treatment exists simultaneously with the right to treatment. The right to obtain treatment does not impose an obligation to accept treatment. Consequently, one can commit a patient who is insane or dangerous to himself or others or unable to care for himself; but one cannot, except in extreme circumstances, compel that patient to participate in a treatment program. His mental condition has not altered to allow him to be released, but he has effectively reduced a psychiatric hospital to a warehouse. Halleck (1980) has characterized the result of recent legal forays into mental health care as a state of increased responsibility and decreased power to discharge those duties. One possible avenue in this bind would be to press for a judicial finding that the patient was also, in fact, incompetent to determine whether or not to utilize treatment as a way of providing therapy.

Criminal Law

The few criminal cases on record involving therapists seem to fall into three possible areas, each related to similar tortious activities. One is criminal negligence, where the action directly caused the death of a patient. Another is rape. This has uniformly been invoked where the sexual contact has occurred between adult therapists and minor patients. Lastly, in theory, a criminal assault and battery action could exist if there was no way to justify the battery as part of therapy, no matter how negligently performed.

Product Liability Law

A new approach to legal liability is emerging from the increased use of machinery, such as electroconvulsive therapy machines or biofeedback equipment, in the practice of psychotherapy. In this area, patients may sue to recover for injuries caused by defective products. The therapist must ensure that the damage was due to a defective product, not defective usage. Then the liability falls on the manufacturer, not the user. At the very least, the therapist ought to (1) be careful in his selection of machines, using only those that meet Food and Drug Administration standards; (2) inspect the machine for patent or outwardly visible defects before any usage; (3) obtain the patient's fully informed consent to use the machine; (4) follow all label warnings and printed instructions; (5) use only those machines that he is trained to operate completely, so that he is able to assess and prevent risks.

Immunity from Suit

Employees of many governmental agencies are protected by "sovereign immunity," which means, in effect, that they cannot be sued. A therapist should ascertain whether the agency employing him is covered by this doctrine and whether the state in which he works recognizes the doctrine. Whether or not a particular agency—for example, probation and parole boards or child protective services—is immune to suit is being decided in a piecemeal and inconsistent fashion in state and federal courts. Where immunity exists, it is not an absolute shield. Exceptions to this immunity occur (1) if the negligent act was beyond the scope of the employee's duties in his job, (2) if the act constituted a case of callous and wanton neglect, and (3) if the act took place in the performance of a ministerial, rather than a discretionary, duty of the employee's job. A ministerial duty is generally defined as an act one performs in a given state of facts in a prescribed manner, in obedience to the mandate of legal authority, without regard to, or the exercise of one's own judgment upon, the propriety of the act being done. Simply put, a duty to be exercised by rote and not judgment is a ministerial act. More specifically, if an act is expressly a part of an agency's policy and is supposed to be routinely performed in all instances, a failure to perform that act is negligence in a ministerial duty. For example, if a search of *all* patients committed to a ward for the criminally insane is mandated by the hospital and an admitting staff member failed to search a patient, who subsequently harmed himself or another patient, such failure would constitute negligence. In contrast, there is a public policy articulated in the courts that public officials should be exempt from liability for errors of judgment, since such officials must constantly make high-risk decisions (for instance, about parole or probation).

Legal Education

Considering the myriad laws generated by case or by statute, and the plethora of administrative regulations, how can one keep current on the legal impact on psychotherapeutic practice? At least annually, one ought to review changes in state statutory law applicable to psychotherapeutic practice. State codebooks are often kept in public libraries, with the current year's revisions in a sleeve in the back of each volume. Case precedent decisions are reported in the regional case reporter for each state. Cases are indexed by key words for easy retrieval and are available at law libraries and bar associations. The laws that have direct impact on a therapist's practices are the ones enacted by statute or case law in the state where he practices or by federal Supreme Court decisions, which are the laws of the land. For example, the *Tarasoff* decision is the law only in California. This does not mean, however, that it can be ignored elsewhere. Rather, a judge will review state precedents first, to see whether guidelines exist for the current case to be decided. Then, if none exist, he will consult other relevant cases to help him think through the issues at hand and benefit from other judges' ruminations before coming to a decision that establishes the precedent for his jurisdiction. Thus, decisions in other states are not binding but may be an important consideration in how other states' judges will decide a case.

In addition to keeping current on statutory laws and case laws, one can attend workshops on legal issues in psychotherapy and can read journals in this area. Among the best are the *Bulletin of the American Academy of Law and Psychiatry*, the *Journal of Law and Psychiatry*, and the *Mental Disability Law Reporter*.

Insurance Issues

Most psychotherapists carry professional liability insurance. However, they carry it as if it were a talisman to protect them from evil. Most therapists do not read their policies to know what the exclusions are, such as the recent change in the American Psychological Association's policy, which no longer covers sexual contact between patient and therapist. Other forms of legal liability may not be covered. There is no coverage for intentional torts that are also crimes. It is against public policy to insure for the commission of a crime, even if the act was not intended as a crime. Constitutional violations and intentional torts that are not crimes also may not be covered. Some therapists go "bare," feeling that, without coverage, they are less attractive targets for a suit. This is a risky practice because an outraged client still might bring suit, and then one would have to pay sizable legal fees and possibly a settlement. Even if less than the six-figure insurance coverage, a settlement of $5,000 or $10,000 is still a substantial windfall. If it were to be taken out of a therapist's savings, or if his income were garnisheed, the effects could be devastating. Currently, at least for psychologists and social workers, $1,000,000 coverage is still available at modest rates, and psychiatrists' rates are still very low compared to those for other medical specialties.

Other therapists may decide not to purchase personal protection because they operate in an agency that has, usually, sovereign immunity or a group policy for all its employees. In such an agency, the therapist and his supervisors and the agency head may *all* be named as codefendants in a suit. It may be to the insurance company's benefit to attempt to show that the employee's behavior fell outside the scope of the insurance policy's coverage, or to break the chain of responsibility and locate the negligence solely within one employee and thereby avoid liability for the agency. A personal policy ensures the therapist that an attorney will argue strenuously for the therapist's own interests. It must be remembered that ultimately the insurance company's lawyer works for the company and will argue *its* interests most strenuously. This may include settling out of court, despite the therapist's objections. Finally, policies need to be reviewed and updated as legal realities change.

In addition to professional liability insurance, practitioners ought to consider office liability insurance for accidents on the premises.

Another form of protection is to operate in a group practice. Doing so provides two benefits from a legal standpoint: increased available coverage for emergencies and ready consultants on difficult cases. If a group is a legal partnership, all partners can be held liable for the negligence of any member. The personal assets of all partners may also be encumbered. If the group is a professional corporation, then one's individual liability is limited. The professional corporation may be sued and any or all of its members found liable, but its individual members' personal assets cannot be encumbered by the suit.

Most therapists are aware of malpractice suits as a hazard of the profession. However, there are numerous other avenues available to the creative attorney. In our consumerist society, probably the two avenues to show the greatest increase in use will be contract law and intentional torts. The astounding increase in suits regarding informed consent in other specialty areas indicates that such suits inevitably will be brought against psychotherapy as a practice.

These two approaches have the advantage for the plaintiff of avoiding the difficulties of establishing a standard of care and, instead, focusing on more clear-cut issues of contractual terms and adequacy of informed consent. The strong movements within and outside the profession for accountability, specificity of terms (witness the problem-oriented record and the CHAMPUS peer review system), cost control, and patients' rights indicate that explicit contracts will be more frequently requested by patients or required of agencies. The isolation of the consulting room has been irrevocably breached. It remains to be seen what the effect of this push for accountability has on clinical efficacy.

2

●●●●●●●●●●●●●●●●●●●●●●●●●●●●●●●

Establishing the Therapeutic Framework

The Patient as Partner

●●●●●●●●●●●●●●●●●●●●●●●●●●●●●●●●

Many risks of legal liability for practicing therapists involve the establishment and maintenance of the therapeutic relationship and the duties imposed by that relationship. Key components of the therapeutic relationship include informed consent to therapy (consent based on the patient's awareness of the diagnosis and treatment choice, including innovative psychotherapies) and contracts in therapy.

Informed Consent

Informed consent plays an important part in determining the outcome of suits for assault and battery (including electroshock and drug treatments), defamation of character, and invasion of privacy. Details of the particular consents are discussed

21

in later chapters; here I focus on the general issue of informed consent, regardless of the content of the consent.

The doctrine of *volenti non fit injuria* ("no wrong is done to one who is willing") describes the defense of consent to intentional conduct that would otherwise be tortious—for example, a battery. However, consent is irrelevant to negligence actions, for what reasonable person would consent to negligent injury? While consent is no defense to a negligence action, the failure to obtain an informed consent is a negligent act in itself.

The situations that most obviously, based on the incidence of suits, call for an informed consent are therapeutic approaches involving physical contact (psychodrama, Gestalt therapy, Rolfing) and drug or electroshock therapy. With traditional verbal therapies, no cases based on the failure to obtain informed consent have been reported. However, Tarshis (1972, p. 89) vividly describes the precedential case: "The patient may submit to a course of treatment without having been told that he must actively participate, that he might during treatment become more manifestly upset than before, that the period of treatment is indefinite, and that his chances of improvement depend to a large extent on his own motivations. If the doctor does not make these explanations of the character of the treatment, and the patient later finds himself unprepared to make the commitment necessary for successful treatment and has suffered emotional harm for which he was unprepared, he could found his actions on lack of consent, without proving that his deterioration was due to the doctor's negligence."

In short, the patient has the right to make an informed consent before undergoing any procedure, and the complementary duty of the therapist is to make whatever disclosure is necessary for the patient to make an informed consent.

Competence to Consent

Consent can be made only by a person legally considered competent to consent. This issue arises first if one is treating a child. Except in cases of emergency, a consent usually should be obtained from the legal guardian of a patient under the age of eighteen (unless the child is married or self-supporting or has been emancipated by a court). In each state, however, certain forms of health care (for example, birth control pills or drug abuse treatment) can be consented to by children under eighteen, without their parents' approval or knowledge. What is allowed varies in each jurisdiction and is usually determined by statute.

Numerous complications arise among parents, child, and therapist when there are disagreements about the necessity of the treatment. An especially troublesome situation arises when the therapist feels that the parents are pushing therapy unnecessarily, to scapegoat a child. In this situation, a clear statement of one's position and an offer to obtain a second opinion seem appropriate. Another thorny situation arises when the parents refuse therapy for an obviously disturbed child. In this situation, the therapist might consider filing a petition of abuse or neglect against the parents, since in many states the refusal to provide needed health care is grounds for a finding of abuse. An independent practitioner who files such a petition might find it prudent not to be the provider of services, since the parents might bring suit for abuse of process. That is, they might charge that the real purpose of the legal process was not to protect the child but to garner fees for the therapist.

Consent also becomes an issue when one is treating a person who is incompetent to consent because of diminished capacity. Incompetence is a legal determination, and the mere presence of "mental illness" does not render one incompetent. If a person has been previously adjudicated as incompetent, then a guardian has been appointed, and the guardian may consent to the treatment. Of the two types of guardians—those of estate and those of person—only the guardian of the person can consent to the treatment of that person. If the person is not incompetent but is seriously impaired by psychological disturbance, a decision must be made whether the person moves in and out of phases of lucidity. If so, and in the absence of an emergency, one might prudently consider delaying treatment until the person recovers the ability to consent. If the person is quite impaired and unlikely to regain lucidity in the absence of treat-

ment, one might consider getting the nearest relative to petition
for guardianship and then to consent to the treatment. There is
a risk entailed when a mentally disturbed patient refuses treatment in a nonemergency situation and the family is not informed of the competency and guardianship laws. If the patient's condition deteriorates or the family suffers losses during
the acute phase of the disturbance—losses that could have been
avoided had they known of the possibility of commitment—
then negligence may be charged.

A second major requirement of the person consenting,
apart from the legal ability to do so, is that the consent be voluntary. There should be no additional inducements or forms of
coercion by the practitioner or institution offering the service.
To the extent that one can be aware of coercive pressures being
applied to the patient by the patient's family, one must consider not accepting that consent as valid until the coercion is
halted. If the family refuses and there is no emergency, one
might refer the patient elsewhere.

What to Disclose

Once a therapist knows that he is dealing with a competent patient, the next question is: What information must be
disclosed to the patient, and how is it to be disclosed? First, the
language must be nontechnical, objective, and designed to be
comprehensible to the patient. The duty to disclose is not satisfied merely by the spewing out of facts, but must be a dialogue
culminating in the patient's understanding. There is quite a difference among jurisdictions as to how much information must
be disclosed. I will outline the areas most frequently cited as
comprising an informed consent and suggest, in light of the current state of research, what one might reasonably say to a patient to convey the necessary information accurately.

Conservatively, a therapist should inform the patient of
the nature of his disorder and should describe the therapeutic
program recommended, indicating also the anticipated benefits
of the program, the foreseeable material risks of the treatment,
and the likely results of no treatment. The therapist also should

describe alternative methods of treatment. If the recommended therapy is experimental, the patient should be informed of that also.

Diagnosis. In reporting a diagnosis to a patient, the therapist should include a disclaimer concerning the reliability and validity of the diagnostic process, since the procedures are often untested for reliability or validity or, where tested, found generally low, allowing for significant variance between diagnosticians. Certain diagnoses carry most risk of legal liability: Is the patient (1) suicidal? (2) dangerous to others? (3) legally insane? (4) Is the symptom picture due to a medical, rather than mental, illness? Similarly, situations where a given diagnosis results in a tangible loss for the patient—commitment hearings, custody hearings, disability determinations—carry increased risk.

To be considered negligent, a diagnosis must be wrong *and* arrived at negligently. Since—as the literature shows—the reliability and validity of our diagnoses are low, it is difficult to determine whether a diagnostic error was the result of negligence or the nature of the diagnostic process itself. Fink (1973) has noted that an erroneous diagnosis will be held to be an error in judgment, not negligence, if the diagnostician can show (1) that reasonable doubt exists concerning the nature of the condition involved; (2) that authorities do not agree on the diagnostic procedures to be used and that one of the acceptable procedures was used; and (3) that the diagnostician made a conscientious effort to inform himself of the patient's condition.

The therapist should request previous treatment records and review these records for what information they shed on other therapists' diagnostic or treatment impressions. Suits charging negligence have been filed for failure to pursue information that on the face of it seemed useful and then turned out to be vital (*Merchants National Bank* v. *U.S.,* 272 F. Supp. 409 (D.N.D. 1967)) and also for the failure to forward significant information from one therapist to another (*Underwood* v. *U.S.,* 356 F.2d 92 (5th Cir. 1966)). In *Merchants National Bank,* a psychiatrist who did not pursue a patient's allegation that her husband intended to harm her was found to be negligent. In *Underwood,* an Air Force psychiatrist, who was being transferred off base, failed to inform his patient's new psychiatrist of that patient's threats against his wife's life. The new therapist allowed the patient, Airman Dunn, to return to duty and draw a firearm, and Dunn used this weapon to kill his wife. Mrs. Dunn's father sued successfully, charging that this failure to forward information constituted negligence.

Probably the single largest area of litigation involving diagnosis is the charge of a wrongful commitment.There are a variety of avenues for the patient to pursue: (1) negligent diagnosis as a malpractice action, (2) malicious prosecution, (3) false imprisonment, (4) defamation of character, (5) breach of confidentiality, (6) invasion of privacy, (7) constitutional rights violation, (8) violation of the right to due process.

Many of the defenses to these actions were spelled out in Chapter One. Briefly, in malicious prosecution, it is very difficult to prove the malicious intent. In defamation of character or libel charges, the defense is truth, which would be shown if the commitment is upheld by the judicial review process; if not, the defense of privilege to give testimony in a legal hearing may hold. False imprisonment is an intentional tort requiring actual imprisonment or commitment without probable cause. It is similar to the negligent diagnosis action of malpractice. In essence, one must show that a reasonable cause existed to make the diagnosis that led to the commitment. Thus, the diagnosis would be true (defense to defamation), and the commitment would be reasonable to protect the patient or society (not an invasion of privacy), done without malice, and in accordance with statutory procedure (due process action). Schwitzgebel and Schwitzgebel (1980) offer a number of guidelines for doing a commitment evaluation:

1. Conduct an examination. Failure to directly examine the patient leaves one wide open to be questioned whether probable cause for commitment existed.
2. Spend some time alone with the patient.
3. Confirm the absence of drugs or consider whether and to what extent they account for the patient's behavior.
4. Conduct or arrange for a physical examination of the pa-

tient to rule out gross physical conditions accounting for the behavior. Some of the highest awards have been made when behavior has been dismissed as psychogenic when subsequent examination revealed organic causes (*Brown* v. *Moore*, 141 F. Supp. 816 (W.D. Pa. 1956), 247 F.2d 711 (3rd Cir. 1957), *Weinshenk* v. *Kaiser Foundation Hospitals*, No. 480278 (Cal. Super. Ct. 1970)).

5. Be accurate in verbatim quotes.

6. In your report, distinguish between what was observed and what was reported by others.

7. Avoid conflict of interest; that is, avoid having a relationship with those committing the patient or with the facility that will receive the patient. (If the therapist is the brother of a woman who is committing her husband, there may be a presumption of bias as a result of the dual relationship. Similarly, if the examining psychiatrist is also a staff member or medical director of the hospital he recommended for treatment, he may be accused of trying to garner fees for the hospital.)

8. Make sure your referral is an appropriate one to a facility equipped to provide the treatment necessary in the least restrictive environment.

9. Be in compliance with all statutory requirements of due process in the examination and filing of papers.

10. Confirm, if possible, a patient's stories about third parties. Hogan (1979) reports that in *Rosario* v. *State*, 274 N.Y.S.2d 81 (1966), 305 N.Y.S. 574 (1969), 372 N.Y.S.2d 647 (1975), Victor Rosario claimed that his wife's lover had cut his arm, drained his blood into a glass, and then had drunk the blood. This story was never checked out, but rather dismissed as a delusion. In fact, it was entirely true.

11. Take a careful history—noting past overt acts, attempts, or threats—in addition to assessing current mental status.

A therapist who is appointed to do a commitment examination has other avenues of immunity from liability. First, there is the majority view that the examining professional is acting in a quasi-judicial or witness role and that it is, in fact, the judge who commits the patient. Second is the majority rule, regarding negligence or malpractice actions, that no duty can be breached because no true doctor-patient or fiduciary relationship ever existed between the examining psychiatrist and the person committed. This is the majority rule, but it is not an absolute shield. (*Majority view* or *majority rule* refers to a tendency for courts throughout the country to decide similar cases in similar ways. The result is that, generally, one may expect that anywhere in the country a court will *probably* view the doctor-patient relationship in this way, although not all courts will do so. A *majority decision* also may refer to a United States Supreme Court decision, which is binding across the country.)

Nature of Therapeutic Process. The description of the therapeutic program may also have clinical benefits, since patients who are told what is going to happen in therapy may be prepared to weather the ambiguities and confusions of this form of human encounter. Divergence of patient-therapist expectations seems strongly related to premature terminations; and pretherapy training, especially on expected role behaviors (see Frank and others, 1978), significantly affects duration of stay.

Treatment Benefits and Risks. As regards the anticipated reasonable benefits, the research literature supports this conclusion: "On the average, psychotherapy is better than no psychotherapy, and . . . above-average therapy often yields excellent results" (Bergin and Lambert, 1978, p. 152). Beyond this, one might consider avoiding a detailed prognosis, which invites a breach of warranty. What are the foreseeable material risks of psychotherapy? First, it must be accepted that there are risks to psychotherapy. Bergin and Lambert (1978, p. 154) surveyed the battlefield of therapy casualties and concluded that "negative effects are widespread enough to influence the general evaluation of psychotherapy." What exactly are the negative effects that may occur? A survey of the injuries cited in malpractice actions shows the following negative effects: loss of a significant relationship (for example, marriage), job, liberty, or constitutional rights; emotional harm; loss of life; invasion of privacy; and/or injury to reputation.

Probably least considered among the foreseeable risks are those associated with confidentiality. One is required to disclose all material risks, or those that a reasonable person would find significant to a decision to undergo therapy. In *amicus* briefs to the California Supreme Court hearing the *Tarasoff* case, the American Psychological Association strongly endorsed the tenet that confidentiality is essential to the trust of the relationship and hence to its success. Therefore, a breach of that confidence, which would throw the efficacy of the treatment into doubt (not including the risk, in some cases, of loss of liberty and damage to reputation engendered by the breach), would seem to constitute a material risk and, with the limits of confidentiality clear in ethical standards and statutes, a foreseeable risk. Therefore, it seems reasonable that part of a discussion of risk would address the limits on confidentiality.

It would therefore be prudent for the psychotherapist to be aware of whatever statutes exist that mandate the disclosure of information. A particular problem exists with group, couples, and family therapy. There are no privilege statutes ensuring the privacy of a patient from disclosures by fellow patients. At the very least, a therapist seeing groups, families, or couples ought to inform them of the need for confidentiality on everyone's part. Exhibit 1 is a sample of the type of contract one might use. Therapists should consult with an attorney before utilizing such a form, to ascertain that it is in accordance with all applicable laws.

Risks of No Treatment. What are the risks of no treatment? According to Bergin and Lambert (1978), approximately 43 percent of neurotic patients show a remission in symptoms within two years. At the same time, "treatment effects of that magnitude are frequently obtained in six months or less of formal psychotherapy" (p. 171). There is, then, "considerable evidence of treatment efficiency/efficacy over no treatment" (p. 171). All of the negative effects of psychotherapy are also foreseeable risks of no treatment: divorce, loss of job, suicide, aggravation of symptoms, depression, psychosis, and so on.

Alternative Modes of Treatment. Regarding alternative modes of psychotherapy, the literature to date, as reviewed by

Exhibit 1. Sample Group Therapy Confidentiality Agreement

Date: _____

    In return for the benefits available from group therapy and in consideration of mutual promises by all other participants, we, the undersigned, agree to hold confidential all communications made by participants while in a group session. Extra-session communications are not covered by this agreement. If confidentiality for such communications is requested, it must be done at the time of the communication. We are aware that certain ethical requirements of the therapist or legal requirements may supersede this agreement. To whatever degree possible, the therapist has specified those conditions to us. We are aware that there exists no judicial privilege for group therapy communications and that whatever is said here may be repeated in a courtroom.

    This agreement is binding on all participants in this therapy group, and any breach of this agreement entitles the offended party to recover for any and all harms which can be proven. This agreement may be altered at any time but only in writing and with the signatures of all participants.

                                                                               _____

  _____

  _____

  _____

  _____

  _____

Bergin and Lambert (1978, p. 170), led them to conclude that the various modes are, on the whole, equally effective: "Psychoanalytic/insight therapies, humanistic or client-centered psychotherapy, many behavior therapy techniques, and, to a lesser degree, cognitive therapy rest on a reasonable empirical base. They do achieve results that are superior to no treatment and to various placebo treatment procedures. . . . Generally, the above schools of therapy have been found to be equally effective with the broad spectrum of outpatients to whom they are typically applied. . . . Although the foregoing is generally true, it seems clear that with circumscribed disorders—such as certain phobias, some sexual dysfunctions, and compulsions—certain behavioral operations can reliably bring about success." Research has not yet specified whether these alternate modes of therapy possess differential types or degrees of risk. However, clinical reports (commented on by Bergin and Lambert, 1978) exist of iatrogenic injuries in insight therapy, behavior therapy, group therapy, family therapy, and couples therapy.

Once one has discussed other modes of therapy, what other alternative helping systems exist? Are such alternatives tantamount to no treatment? Do they illustrate Eysenck's concept of "spontaneous remission" occurring in the absence of "formal" psychotherapy? We do not know whether any particular group of such services is more efficient or less risky than therapy, and this ought to be said. Also, patients should be told that they can get some form of help by going to classes or church, by utilizing personal effectiveness training programs (Parent Effectiveness Training, Transcendental Meditation, Assertiveness, Yoga, Relaxation), or by participating in peer self-help groups (Alcoholics Anonymous, Parents Without Partners, Parents Anonymous, Recovery, Inc., disability support groups). If a patient is facing a crisis and does not have a long-standing difficulty, specialized resources such as rape crisis centers and battered-wife shelters may help her through a short-term crisis more effectively than the individual practitioner can.

Innovative Therapies. A therapist who uses a form of treatment that is innovative for its time must be prepared to justify his decision if a negative outcome ensues. One such justification might be that the treatment had previously been submitted to testing under research conditions. Another justification might be that the therapist had exhausted all other treatment approaches with a particular patient.

What constitutes an innovative therapy? Generally, the dynamic insight therapies, the humanistic relationship-based therapies, and the behavioral and cognitive therapies would not now be considered innovative. They stand on a substantial base of empirical studies and scholarship and have been used to treat a variety of problems. (Therapists using any of these approaches, however, should ascertain whether the literature indicates its prior use with a certain problem or expressly delineates contraindicated populations.) More risky are the various therapies utilizing physical contact (including sexual intercourse) as means of fostering change in personality, as well as the therapies utilizing cathartic or emotional flooding processes. The physical contact therapies run the risk of creating physical injuries or offensively touching a patient. The cathartic therapies run the risk of overwhelming the patient and contributing to a decompensation or other form of noxious psychological process.

At one time, the common view of therapy was such that any physical contact between patient and therapist was looked at askance, as the therapist acting out. In *Hammer* v. *Rosen,* 181 N.Y.S.2d 805 (1959), 198 N.Y.S.2d 65 (1960), John Rosen, M.D., the developer of the direct analytic method of psychotherapy, was sued for negligence by a patient's parents, who alleged—among other charges—that he had assaulted her. The court accepted an argument by the plaintiff's attorneys of a prima facie case of malpractice in Dr. Rosen's use of physically confrontive embodiments of the patient's inner psychic conflicts. This decision that the acts were obviously negligent (or at least so innovative as to generate considerable anxiety in the public's mind) cast the burden of proof on the defendant, changing the balance of the case. Rather than the plaintiff's proving negligence, the defendant must now prove the reasonableness of his action. Dawidoff (1973b) infers that Rosen made the tactical judgment that his entire therapeutic approach might fail with this adjudication and that the methodology could be preserved if the case were tried on the grounds of denial of the primary complaint. That is, he elected not to raise the possibility that therapy *with a consent* could involve what would otherwise be illegal batteries and that physical contact between therapist and patient was not per se grounds for negligence. Instead, he chose to deny the parents' primary allegation. (The New York Supreme Court found that a cause of action existed in this case. Whether the case ever went back to trial or was settled out of court is unknown.)

Generally, suits against innovative therapies have been based on negligence in techniques, assault and batteries (apprehension of and/or harmful or offensive touching without consent), or infliction of emotional duress. Successful suits have been brought for physical injuries that occurred in encounter-type groups utilizing physical exercises between participants (*Annis* v. *Donahue*, No. 303295 (D. Mass. 1969), *Grant* v. *National Training Laboratories*, No. 350570 (D.C. Cir. 1970), *Borker* v. *National Training Laboratories*, No. 69-4793 (S.D.N.Y. 1969)).

Clearly, screening patients for high-risk forms of therapy is essential. Unfortunately, we are just beginning to research therapist and patient characteristics and interactions that lead to therapeutic casualties.

The easiest defense to a suit for assault and battery is to obtain an informed consent for the touching. A consent is not an absolute shield, for the touching must not exceed that which was consented to. In *Abraham* v. *Zaslow*, No. 245862 (Cal. Super. Ct. June 30, 1972), the patient, Ms. Abraham, apparently had seen films of Dr. Zaslow's new "Z-therapy" being done with autistic children. However, she was not prepared by that exposure for a session where, as Hogan (1979) reports, she was poked and beaten and battered while restrained by strangers for more than ten hours. The resulting injuries, including alleged renal failure, were compensated by an award of $170,000.

Apart from intentional physical contact, such as Rolfing and psychodrama, there are also occasions of unforeseen physical contacts between patients and therapists. Most frequent of these is the physical restraint of child or adolescent patients and less frequently of adults. Self-defense, the prevention of harm to others, or the prevention of substantial damage to property is a valid defense to an assault and battery action. However, one cannot use excessive force—only the minimum necessary to control the person and end the threatened risk to others. When physically restraining a child, one is exposed to a second risk: if excess force is used, an action for child abuse—as well as a battery suit—may follow. Since therapists are usually of the class of adults entrusted with care of children (along with teachers and

daycare providers), their abuse of that care may—by statute—
constitute child abuse.

The riskiest form of physical contact between patient and
therapist is sexual contact. Almost without exception, this is
the only area where criminal sanctions have been invoked. Various actions are available in recourse to the patient in such a situation. The situation described here is that where the sexual
contact was mutually consented to and free of overt coercion or
force, which would constitute rape. Instead, the personal lever-
age of the relationship, the idealizing transference, and the patient's dependency are used to justify a sexual component to
the therapy.

The criminal cases on record (*People* v. *Bernstein,* 171
Cal. App. 2d 279 (1959), *People* v. *Silverman* (Va. 1979)) have
all been statutory rape charges resulting from sexual relations
between adult therapists and minor clients. Most frequently in
this area, an adult patient will bring charges of malpractice or
battery. If the patient is married, the spouse may bring suit for
alienation of affection, seduction, or criminal conversation. The
spouse, however, may not be able to bring a civil action for
these offenses, since many states have passed "heart-balm statutes" barring such action. Battery suits also are hard to win because generally there is an element of consent on the part of the
patient. Malpractice, hence, is the likeliest avenue of recovery.
Using this approach, the plaintiff is trying to show that the therapist's behavior fell below the minimum standard of care. Since
such behavior is clearly proscribed by ethical code and licensing
statute and is roundly denounced in the professional literature,
a breach of duty is likely to be found if the plaintiff can prove
that the offense occurred (no mean feat without witnesses).
This is one area of malpractice litigation where there is as close
to a consensus on the standard of care as one is likely to see.
The major problem is proving that the acts actually took place.

Therapists have generally tended to use two defenses,
neither one very successfully. The first is that the sex was a part
of the therapy. An example is the defense offered in *Cooper* v.
California Board of Medical Examiners, D. 1329 (Cal. Super. Ct.
1972): "Dr. Cooper is a firm believer in the fact that the body

has a tremendous significance and influence on our actions; and the awareness of one's body is one of the keys to personal health; mental health; and his techniques may be considered new, revolutionary, and even bizarre perhaps to some people. But none of us knows the potential of the human body in relation to the human mind, and to explore that and make a person whole is Dr. Cooper's dedicated professional goal." Overwhelmingly, the courts have tended to view sex as acting out of the countertransference and hence negligent.

The second line of defense is that the sexual relationship was a separate one from the therapeutic relationship or process and did not impinge on the therapeutic process; hence, there could be no professional negligence or malpractice. It has not been a very successful defense, since courts are reluctant to accept such a compartmentalized view of human relationships. A therapist attempting to prove the legitimacy of sexual relations between himself and a patient by establishing that two coterminous-in-time but utterly parallel relations existed has a difficult task. Since the suit most likely will be instituted by the patient, she will present strong evidence that the therapy relationship led to her consent to the sex and that the sexual relationship then spilled back and contaminated the therapy process. Even if that defense is accepted, then a second difficulty arises; namely, that, even with the consent, the fiduciary role of the therapist flatly rules out using the relationship to one's own gain, and the picture of a self-sacrificing therapist bravely undergoing repeated doses of ungratifying sex solely for the patient's benefit is too much to swallow.

Two interesting theoretical possibilities do exist. First, in the initial contract—with a fully informed consent of benefits, risks, experimentality of procedure, alternatives, and so on—the therapist might have received a consent for sex to be the mode of treatment. The argument of a mishandling of the transference would be difficult to show, since the consent would predate the development of the transference, and battery would be voided by the consent. The fiduciary role and its constraints would probably be the only recourse to show negligence, since even though the ward may consent to gain by the guardian, the guardian must forgo that benefit. The second possible justification is that the therapeutic approach is a nontransferential one—for example, behavior modification, where the patient-therapist relationship is not seen as involved in the change process, so that separate relationships (again with a consent) would be a possibility.

Recent decisions have raised the possibility that egregious behavior, including sexual relations with patients, may be so outlandish as to be inconceivable as therapy and hence unrecoverable as the malpractice of therapy. The patient may prove too much. The Missouri State Supreme Court's decision in *Zipkin* v. *Freeman*, 436 S.W.2d 753 (Mo. 1968), illustrates this reasoning: "Many of the acts of Dr. Freeman did not constitute malpractice nor did they have any true relationship with professional services. . . . This relationship passed the point at which anyone could logically believe that [the acts] had any reasonable connection with professional services or that they were being performed in the course of any legitimate treatment." Here, then, the tort approach found no liability because the therapist was not practicing his profession but was engaged in some other form of human endeavor. However, a contract approach—based on the existence of an implied contract with fiduciary obligations of faithful and diligent care—might find liability precisely because the therapist was not practicing. If he was not practicing, why was he taking money during the contacts?

In *Roy* v. *Hartogs*, 366 N.Y.S.2d 297 (Civ. Ct. 1975), 381 N.Y.S.2d 587 (1976), the tort approach did find liability. However, when Dr. Hartogs then sued his insurance company (*Hartogs* v. *Employers Mutual Liability Insurance Co. of Wisconsin*, 89 Wisc. 2d 468 (1977)) for refusing to pay the damages in the malpractice judgment against him for his sexual relationship with Julie Roy, the court ruled that Dr. Hartogs could not recover from his carrier because he had claimed that his actions were not therapy and therefore not the malpractice of therapy. If the patient believed that the actions were therapy, the court added, she could sue the insurance company to recover for any injuries that she received. Thus, the patient's mind controls, at least in New York.

Riskin (1979) suggests that therapists who are serious about justifying sex as therapy for competent adult patients would do well to submit a research protocol, similar to that required by Department of Health and Human Services regulations, to be approved by the appropriate state and federal review board. This would protect them, and the research might provide an answer to questions such as "Can sex be therapeutic?" "For what types of disorders?" "What kind of sex for what kind of patient administered by what kind of therapist?" "What are the risks of 'bad' sex?"

The question always arises: What about the blameless therapist, unjustly accused by the delusional or vindictive patient? How can he best protect himself? First, he should be impeccable in all contacts with clients and do nothing that presents even the appearance of misconduct. He should maintain the integrity of the professional relationship and do nothing to blur the boundaries with other forms of contact with the patient. The patient is then left only with her version of what happened alone behind closed doors—without, for example, the supporting evidence that, yes, she and the therapist were seen together having a drink, no matter how innocent. The appearance of misconduct is difficult to overcome, and an unnecessary risk to take. If the therapy involves certain "social contacts," such as home visits or phobia desensitization sessions, a third party should be present as an observer.

There are also legal risks in sex therapy clinics where sexual surrogates are used for therapy purposes. Leroy (1972) has outlined the manifold risks. The possible criminal charges include:

1. Prostitution, if the surrogate is paid.
2. Adultery, if the patient is married; unlawful fornication, if the patient is single.
3. Pimping, pandering, and procuring charges against the employing therapists and the clinic, provided the surrogate sets up the contact or makes money from the sexual transaction.
4. Operating a house of prostitution, if the clinic allows the sex therapy to be consummated on its grounds; or a Mann

Act violation, if the patient and surrogate cross a state line in search of a place to consummate the relationship.

Leroy then offers the following suggestions for avoiding these legal risks. First, one should treat only married couples, if possible, thereby removing the surrogates from the program entirely. But what of the needs of the sexually dysfunctional single person? First, a single surrogate should be used, to avoid adultery charges by the surrogate's spouse. Second, unpaid volunteers should be used as surrogates, so that all the risks except for an unlawful fornication charge are removed.

Since this is an unlikely arrangement, one might prudently move to integrate the surrogates, if paid, as much as possible into the treatment team by daily consultation, follow-up counseling, and formal training. The surrogates might be placed in other positions in the treatment facility for some time and then put back into the field. As much as possible, one should avoid the image of providing a prostitute who services the client and then disappears. If the surrogates are involved in other aspects of the treatment, so that their function, while it includes sex, is not only sex, the credibility of the idea that the sex is part of the therapy is increased, and the person cannot be seen as solely a sex partner, but a legitimate member of the treatment team.

Consent Forms

After the therapist has presented all the relevant information, he should be available to answer patient inquiries and to confirm that the patient understands what he has been told. If a patient has significant reservations, he should be allowed a few days to consider the situation and come to a decision. When the patient does consent to treatment, the therapist might ask him to sign a consent form. Written, signed forms primarily have evidentiary value to prove that a proper consent was obtained. The written consent should include an acknowledgment, above the patient's signature, with at least the elements shown in Exhibit 2.

This written acknowledgment should be witnessed by a disinterested third party. Again, before use of such a form, one

Exhibit 2. Sample Informed Consent Form

My signature affirms that Dr. _____ has disclosed to me in simple, nontechnical language the nature of the therapy, including the material risks and benefits, the alternatives available to me, and the risks of no treatment. This disclosure was understood by me and enabled me to make an informed voluntary consent to this treatment. I understand that I may revoke this consent at any time without penalty.

should consult with an attorney regarding its compliance with all applicable laws.

Therapeutic Privilege

There are certain situations where an informed consent need not be obtained. The therapeutic privilege to withhold information can be invoked, first of all, in an emergency. Here, treatment should be limited to that necessary to control the emergency, and, if possible, consent by a guardian or relative should be obtained. Second, one may withhold information if he believes that disclosure of the risks of the treatment might unduly alarm the patient and cause him to reject a minimally risky treatment. Third, if the therapist believes that the disclosure will increase the risk of the treatment, by affecting the patient's psychological makeup and thereby precipitating an emotional harm or significantly reducing his ability to use the therapy, the therapist may decide against disclosure.

Once a therapist invokes the therapeutic privilege, he must accept the burden of proof that a full disclosure would have harmed the patient. Otherwise, he faces a potential charge that the incomplete disclosure was abuse of duty. On the other hand, if he does make a full disclosure, he faces the charge that the statements given caused an injury or caused the patient to refuse a treatment and that, as a result, the patient suffered an injury.

Contracts

The duties of the therapist derive from a fiduciary role, not a contract. The doctrine of *caveat emptor* ("let the buyer beware") is obviated by this fiduciary relationship. However, there is also a contractual side to the relationship because it is a fee-for-services arrangement. The patient may feel he is not getting his money's worth from the therapist. One way to decrease the ambiguity in the relationship that gives rise to that concern is to use an explicit contract.

Schwitzgebel and Schwitzgebel (1980, p. 283) write, "It is doubtful, however, that a research or therapy contract could serve as a release for claims based on negligence." One cannot contract for negligence, nor will an exculpatory contract be honored. One cannot execute a contract that is a bar to all liability. Such contracts are generally not considered legally binding because of their vagueness and because of the unequal bargaining position of the two parties. The inequality in bargaining in a therapy contract springs from the disparity in knowledge between therapist and patient, and the patient's duress and perhaps greater felt need for the therapist than vice versa. A comprehensive informed consent form, which includes information about the relative ease of access to other therapists, might help to equalize the position of the patient and therapist and hence make the contract more valid. Informing the patient of the access to other therapists makes clear that this is not an adhesion contract with a unique service provider. If the patient later decides that his "mental illness" made him unable to enter into the contract, he will face a prodigious task in proving that assertion, for the standards of incompetence to enter into a contract are very high.

The contract describes what the therapist will provide, but it does not promise that that service will lead to a cure. (A therapist is not a guarantor of cure unless he takes that duty on himself. The failure to deliver then constitutes a breach of warranty.) Apart from negligence, a therapist may perform up to the standard of care and still not be helpful. The contract will provide clarity as to whether or not the therapist provided the service he promised, regardless of the outcome.

Contracts generally include the following elements:

1.   Focus of the therapy (behavior and/or feeling states).

2. Procedures to be used (for example, interpretation, confrontation, guided imagery, touching, or meditating).
3. Desired and likely outcome and, if possible, the methods to be used to assess the outcome.
4. If a separate informed consent form is not being used, an explanation of material foreseeable risks, including limits of confidentiality.
5. Fees for specific services and cancellation policy.
6. A statement that this contract can be renegotiated or terminated at any time without penalty.

The use of a contract assists in developing an individualized treatment plan for a patient. The therapist also needs to remember the mandate to provide services in the least restrictive manner. A sample contract is shown in Exhibit 3. Because numerous aspects of state law delineate the nature of professional relationships, one should consult an attorney prior to use of this or any other contract form.

The use of a contract is a double-edged sword. If the therapist's actions fall within the scope of the contract, it is a protection from liability. If they fall outside the scope of the contract, the road to assignment of liability is much clearer for the plaintiff. Utilizing a contract removes one of negligence law's most beneficial (for the defendant) aspects—its vagueness. The determination of a standard of care by one's peers in a field where, to date, hundreds of schools of psychotherapy exist is replaced by the narrower question of whether or not the therapist did what he promised to do.

Exhibit 3. Psychotherapy Contract

I, ____Dr. Schutz____, agree to meet with _____ each _____ at _____ beginning on _____. During these _____ minute sessions, we will direct our mutual efforts toward these goals:

1. _____
2. _____
3. _____

Each goal may not be addressed in each and every session.

The following techniques will be utilized to facilitate attaining these goals:

1. _____
2. _____
3. _____

Progress toward these goals and the presence of potential negative effects will be monitored in the following ways:

1. _____
2. _____

____Dr. Schutz____ and _____ agree to renegotiate or terminate this contract at any time. We include the possibility that the goals and treatment processes may need to be changed at any time. _____ understands that this agreement does not guarantee the attainment of these goals, but rather that ____Dr. Schutz____ will apply his/her professional skills in good faith at all times.

_____ agrees to pay _____ dollars per session. The fee is due at _____.

If an appointment is canceled with less than _____ hours' notice, there will be a charge for that session. The only exceptions to this rule are:

1. _____
2. _____

Generally, third-party payers do not reimburse for missed appointments. Missed appointments are so noted on the bill.

_____'s signature affirms that he/she has been informed in simple, nontechnical terms of the likely benefits and material risks of this treatment plan, the risks of no treatment, and the available alternative treatments. His/Her signature also affirms his/her voluntary assent to the treatment plan.

We further stipulate that this agreement become a part of the record, which is accessible to both parties at will but to no other person without _____'s written consent. ____Dr. Schutz____ will respect _____'s right, within limits by statutory law or ethical code, to the confidentiality of any information communicated by him/her during the course of therapy. _____ has been informed of these limits on confidentiality.

_____
Client's (or guardian's) signature

_____
Therapist's signature

_____
Date

3

●●●●●●●●●●●●●●●●●●●●●●●●●●●●●●●●

Managing the Therapeutic Relationship

The Therapist as Trustee

●●●●●●●●●●●●●●●●●●●●●●●●●●●●●●●●●

The preceding chapter, with its emphasis on informed consent and contracts, revealed the law's equalitarian view of the therapist-patient relationship. The law has attempted to get the patient placed on an equal footing with the therapist by mandating that patients must have access to all the information necessary to decide whether treatment is in their best interests. After that initial phase where the therapeutic framework is established, the law returns to the view of the therapist as trustee, who must look out for the best interests of the patient at all times in the management of the therapy.

Five areas of the management of the therapy relationship carry special risk: (1) response to patient dissatisfaction, (2) charges of undue influence, (3) the duty to get consultation or supervision, (4) duties at termination, and (5) keeping adequate records.

Patient Dissatisfaction

When therapists respond inadequately to patient dissatisfaction, they face a possible lawsuit. *Hess* v. *Frank,* 367 N.Y.S.2d 30 (1975), dealt with the therapist's use of abusive language in discussing a fee dispute. This was not held as an act of misconduct, partly because it did not occur in a session. However, if it had occurred in a session, and if the therapist's behavior had led to a premature termination and emotional damage, it might have been seen as negligence.

Commentators in this area often cite the therapist's skill at handling patient hostility and disappointment as crucial for avoiding suits. Some aspects of patient dissatisfaction are largely due to the patient's "pathology"; for example, borderline idealization and devaluation or paranoid mistrust. However, not all areas of dissatisfaction can be dismissed as the patient's problem. Therefore, therapists should confront all dissatisfactions early, openly, and directly. They should hear the patient out and try to determine whether elements of their own behavior might be contributing to the patient's feelings. If after such an effort a patient is still dissatisfied, one might consider consulting another therapist (either with the patient or alone) or referring the patient to another therapist for treatment.

Undue Influence

Suits charging undue influence—where a third party alleges that the therapist is exercising undue influence over a patient and therefore abusing the relationship—have rarely been brought in the past, partly because therapy was largely nondirective. The advent of the newer directive, problem-solving types of therapy, where the therapist clearly tells the patient what to do, may lead to an increase in this type of suit (in addition to making the causal links of proximate cause easier to establish).

This action is most likely to arise (1) when family members protest because a patient bestows a lavish gift on the therapist or leaves his estate to the therapist; (2) when a patient's spouse, following a move for a separation or divorce, accuses the therapist of alienation of affection; or (3) when a parent accuses a therapist of suggesting certain courses of action to a minor, against the parent's wishes.

In the area of patient bequests to the therapist, Shaffer (1969) describes four possible forms of undue influence:

1. Conscious manipulation of the transference by therapists to their own gain. This is the clearest example of undue influence. It may be pursued as negligence or as fraud. Fraud theory involves false representation, and a conscious manipulation of transference is the false presentation of an offer to help another in order to gain property for oneself. (This argument may also be applied in cases of sexual contact with a patient.)
2. The therapist is aware of the positive transference, is aware of the patient's intention to bestow a gift, and fails to dissuade the patient. Here the issue is clearly one of possible fiduciary abuse. The majority rule on these cases is that no justification is required unless *overt* activity can be proven. However, a minority rule asserts that a presumption of undue influence ought to exist in every confidential relationship and that the fiduciary bears the burden of proving otherwise. Therapists would stand on better ground if they actively tried to dissuade their patients—even if unsuccessfully—from giving a gift. Does this mean that a therapist should never accept a gift from a patient? No. Sometimes, and particularly with children, to do so may rupture the relationship itself. Whenever the gift is substantial, however, the therapeutic impact of acceptance or rejection must be weighed against the potential for abuse.
3. Unconscious manipulation of the transference for personal gain. (Such a charge, however, would be nearly impossible to prove.)
4. No manipulation, but evidence exists of a transference that led, in part, to the bequest.

Clearly, therapists are on the soundest ground if they

steadfastly refuse to act in any way that directly or solely benefits themselves. If they are aware of a bequest or similar actions
taken by the patient, they should dissuade the patient from
such actions.

The other possible cases of undue influence hinge largely on the question of whether the therapist has a duty to
spouses or parents of patients. In all the reported cases, except
one, the therapist, subsequently or concurrently with the therapy that contributed to the dissolution of marriage, was involved personally with the patient. The sole exception is *Salter
v. Grant,* reported in Hogan (1979), where the patient charged
that the therapy had exacerbated his estrangement from his
wife.

As a conservative measure, whenever one is treating a person who reports, as part of the presenting problems, marital difficulties, one might offer to see the other party at least once. If
the spouse refuses a visit, that should be noted in the chart,
along with any comments, such as "That talking stuff doesn't
do any good, anyway."

I am unaware of any parent-child undue influence cases,
so at this time they exist only as theoretical possibilities. The-
oretically, then, in family therapy the family members may
have conflicting goals, and the therapist's theory of family functioning may be at odds with certain members' goals. In such instances, various family members, each disgruntled over different
aspects of the outcome, might bring suit. The juggling of such
disparate goals is quite a feat. The law itself is struggling to delineate the prerogatives of parents and the rights of children and
is having a very difficult time doing so. A therapist's view of the
appropriate solution to that issue may fall outside that determined by his state's statutes or case law. Therefore, he should
keep abreast of his jurisdiction's current decisions on children's
rights and parents' prerogatives before suggesting actions that
fly in the face of statutory directives. If he does proceed with
such actions, he should at least inform family members of their
legal rights and explain that his directives may require that some
of these rights be modified in the interest of therapeutic goals.
For example, a therapist might feel that teenagers have the right

to sexual expression, birth control, and abortion, and he may attempt to pass these values on to the family. However, the law in the state may clearly specify at what age these rights begin (at fourteen or sixteen or eighteen years). Therefore, unless he is careful, a therapist may be suggesting that the parents waive their rights. Patients might well be advised of the legal status of a therapist's suggestions about children's rights. The fact that they were given such information would help to establish that an informed consent was obtained, if the parents should later be displeased at the outcome.

Consultation and Supervision

When therapy reaches a prolonged impasse, the therapist ought to consider consulting another therapist and possibly transferring the patient. Apart from the clinical and ethical considerations, his failure to seek another opinion might have legal ramifications in the establishment of proximate cause in the event of a suit. While therapists are not guarantors of cure or improvement, extensive treatment without results could legally be considered to have injured the patient; in specific, the injury would be the loss of money and time, and the preclusion of other treatments that might have been more successful. To justify a prolonged holding action at a plateau, the therapist would have to show that this was maintaining a condition against a significant and likely deterioration. Consultation at this point would establish the reasonableness of one's approach and help establish criteria for when to terminate one's efforts to treat a patient.

In addition to consultation, a therapist may seek out supervision, or have it required by insurance reimbursement demands, agency policy, licensing regulations, or student status. When one undertakes to supervise the work of another therapist, one also assumes a legal liability not only for one's own acts but for those of the supervisee. Legal liability rests on the de facto or de jure (actual or mandated by law) control the supervisor has over the therapy process to coordinate, direct, and inspect the actions of the treating therapist.

According to the doctrine of *respondeat superiore* ("let the master answer"), the supervisee is not absolved of responsibility; but there is now an additional liable party. Full damages may be recovered from any defendant; thus, a patient may sue the entire line of supervisors in order to increase his chance of getting a recovery. If the master is not negligent but must pay damages, he may then sue the supervisee to recover these damages, under the subrogation doctrine.

One of the major difficulties in psychotherapy supervision is monitoring and maintaining the distinction between errors in treatment and truly destructive behavior. The therapist is in supervision because he is making errors or is of such status that it is expected that he will be making errors. If the errors become actively destructive, the supervisor must intervene to protect the patient.

Another difficulty in supervision, from a risk management perspective, is the fact that most supervision is conducted with the material the supervisee selects to bring to the supervisor. Thus, if behavior goes on that is not being reported to the supervisor, it is beyond the purview of control of the supervisor, though the supervisor still may be found liable. The same lack of control exists in regard to whether or not the therapist is actually carrying out the supervisor's suggestions. Haley (1976) has persuasively argued, for clinical reasons, for live supervision of therapists. From a liability standpoint, this direct observation removes certain major blind spots through which supervisor liability might enter.

Slovenko (1980) points out the following major areas of liability for a supervisor:

1. The supervisor failed to provide information necessary for the therapist to obtain an informed consent or to provide an adequate disclosure to a patient, particularly one undergoing a somatic treatment.
2. In the negligent diagnosis or certification of dangerousness, suicidal intent, legal insanity, or mental illness itself, the supervisor failed to catch the error or else made the misdiagnosis himself.

3. A negligent treatment plan is devised or treatment is carried out beyond its effectiveness, and the supervisor is responsible for the error or does not detect it.
4. The supervisor fails to determine that a new therapist needs to be assigned, treatment terminated, or specialists consulted.
5. The therapist is involved socially or sexually with the patient or exerts undue influence on the patient and conceals his actions from the supervisor.
6. The patient's record does not contain adequate information about the care that the patient has received, and the supervisor does not review the record and have it improved.
7. Negligent supervision occurs in that the supervisor does not meet regularly with the therapist, review the presented material, or elicit necessary information to adequately supervise the case.
8. The therapist is negligent in caring for the patient—for example, he did not adequately supervise a suicidal patient; he released a dangerous patient prematurely; or he failed to provide coverage in his absence—and the supervisor failed to review and approve these decisions.

Basically, any major decision the therapist makes ought to have been reviewed—and modified, if necessary—by the supervisor. The supervisor should foresee what decisions will need to be made or what reasonable options exist, so that if the therapist does not bring up these matters, the supervisor will be able to. Slovenko (1980) reports that in *Cohen* v. *State of New York,* 382 N.Y.S.2d 128 (1976), a first-year psychiatric resident determined that the patient, a documented suicide risk, could be released from the ward to which he was assigned. The patient committed suicide that day. The court determined that a resident "did not at this point in his medical career possess the requisite skill or trained psychiatric judgment to, essentially unsupervised, provide ordinary and reasonable psychiatric medical treatment and care to this decedent." In essence, the resident was allowed to make a decision beyond his capacity, and that decision went without review or approval by a supervisor.

If a supervisor takes on a therapist as a supervisee without checking out his training, license status, previous job recommendations, and previous supervisors' reports, and the supervisee turns out to be grossly incompetent, the supervisor may be liable under the tort of negligent entrustment. The supervisor *should have known* whether his supervisee was qualified to practice at all, even with supervision.

Probably the riskiest situation arises when psychiatrists sign a form attesting to the supervision of a social worker that they never performed, so that the social worker can get insurance reimbursement for that treatment. By signing the form, the supervisor assumes full legal liability but is deprived of any of the protection that really supervising the work would have provided. A New Jersey case reported by Slovenko (1980) involved just this situation. In this case, which was settled out of court, a psychiatrist signed a social worker's written statement that a certain patient—who subsequently killed his wife and children— was not dangerous, although the psychiatrist had never interviewed the patient.

Termination and Abandonment

Once a patient makes a contact with a therapist and the therapist agrees to see him, he is that therapist's patient. The therapist then assumes the fiduciary duty not to abandon the patient. At the very least, therefore, he must refer the patient to another therapist if he elects to terminate the relationship.

Termination of treatment can be of three varieties: (1) Both the therapist and the patient agree that the patient has no further need for services. (2) The patient may decide to terminate but the therapist feels it is unwise. In such a case, the therapist can only explain his feelings and inform the patient about the risk of premature termination; if the patient still refuses, the therapist cannot pursue treatment (except in an emergency). (3) The patient may wish to continue but the therapist may feel that he can no longer help the patient. In this case, the therapist should give adequate notice of the reason for the termination and should help the patient find acceptable alternative services. According to public policy, the therapist has an absolute right to terminate a relationship unilaterally. The relationship is based on mutual trust and rapport; if for any reason the therapist loses rapport with his patient, the basis of the relationship is gone, and the parties must be allowed to separate and seek the requisite relationship elsewhere.

Abandonment, as a breach of fiduciary duty, may be charged (1) when a therapist goes on vacation or is otherwise absent from his practice or (2) when a therapist fails to respond to "emergencies." On vacations or other out-of-town absences, one should arrange for coverage of his clients by a colleague who is competent to handle their particular needs and who has been adequately informed of their status. This requires consent from the patient to release information. (Emergency coverage is discussed further in Chapter Five, on the suicidal patient.)

A potential risk for a suit based on an abandonment charge lies in the use of a telephone-answering machine. If the machine cannot be remotely triggered to play back its messages, the therapist may be out of contact and unreachable for a number of hours. If the therapist does not respond to an emergency call because he has not returned to play back his messages and is therefore unaware of the emergency, he may be open to a charge of abandonment.

Records

Record keeping, from a liability perspective, is a compilation of evidence of the adequacy of care a patient has received. This idea is summarized in the axiom that "work not written is work not done." In fact, an inadequate record has been determined to be negligent in itself (*Whitree* v. *State of New York*, 290 N.Y.S.2d 486 (1968)), in that such a record does not provide a direction for adequate care in the absence of the therapist, and essentially contributes nothing useful to the treatment history of a patient—information that could have a significant bearing on the kind of subsequent care a patient receives.

A good record should include the following items:

1. Written and signed informed consents for all treatment.
2. Written and signed informed consents for all transmissions of confidential information.

3. Treatment contracts, if used.
4. Notes of all treatment contacts made, either in person or by phone, including description of significant events.
5. Notes of all contacts with significant others, or consultations, including correspondence.
6. A complete history and symptom picture leading to a diagnosis, including past and present psychological and psychiatric evaluations, medical history, and a current physical examination. The diagnosis should be reviewed and revised regularly.
7. All prescriptions and a current drug usage profile.
8. A record of the therapist's reasoning as he made all decisions in the diagnosis and treatment of the patient.
9. Any instructions, suggestions, or directives made to the patient that the patient failed to follow through on. (Such records can be used to establish contributory negligence—a powerful defense to any negligence suit.)

Records should not contain subjective or speculative material, and only minimal detail of patient fantasies or dynamic hypotheses should be in the records. However, this speculative material may be kept in a separate "personal therapist's notes" file, as recommended by the American Psychiatric Association Task Force on Confidentiality and now realized by law in Illinois and Washington, D.C. The utter sanctity of these notes has been upheld twice in Illinois court tests.

Records should not be disposed of until the statute of limitations expires. In this connection, one should remember that minor clients' right to sue begins when they come of age and then runs for the duration of the statute of limitations.

The therapist as trustee, then, has duties to consult, to get supervision, to terminate treatment when unproductive, and to keep adequate records for review. The endless analysis that proceeds in isolation is a disappearing phenomenon. The recent move toward peer review by CHAMPUS serves as a mandated consultation in agreement with the tendency of the law to allow others to review a professional's services.

4

●●●●●●●●●●●●●●●●●●●●●●●●●●●●●●●●●●●●

The Dangerous Patient

Tarasoff *and Beyond*

●●●●●●●●●●●●●●●●●●●●●●●●●●●●●●●●●●●●

The *Tarasoff* Case

Tarasoff v. *Regents of the University of California,* 33 Cal. 3d 275 (1973), 529 P.2d 553 (1974), 551 P.2d 334 (1976), is probably the single most widely discussed case in the area of legal liability for psychotherapy. This case pitted the patient's right to privacy against the therapist's duty to protect members of society. Many therapists believe that the decisions in this case served to threaten the sanctity of the therapeutic relationship and to convert the therapist into a policeman, more concerned with keeping the peace than with healing troubled minds.

Briefly, in the *Tarasoff* case, Prosenjit Poddar confided to his therapist his intention to harm Tatiana Tarasoff. Convinced of the seriousness of the threat, his therapist consulted with two

psychiatrists and arranged to have the police detain Poddar as
the first step of a commitment, according to the requirements
of California's Lanterman-Petris-Short Act. The police felt that
Poddar was lucid and accepted his promise to stay away from
Tatiana. Poddar never returned to treatment and two months
later shot and stabbed Tatiana Tarasoff to death:

> The parents brought action against the university
> regents, the police, and doctors in the university hospital,
> charging that defendants negligently permitted Poddar to
> be released from custody without notifying [them] ...
> that their daughter was in grave danger. The superior
> court, Alameda County, found for the defendants, where-
> upon the parents of Tatania appealed. The Supreme
> Court of California reversed the judgment and found the
> defendants guilty of negligence on a charge of "failure to
> warn." The court noted that a psychotherapist treating a
> dangerous client, just as a doctor treating physical illness,
> bears a duty to give threatened persons such warnings as
> are essential to avert foreseeable danger arising from his
> patient's condition or treatment. The California court
> spoke directly to limitations of privileged communications.
> The court stated, "Public policy favoring protection of
> the confidential character of patient-psychotherapist rela-
> tionship must yield in instances in which disclosure is
> essential to avert danger to others; the protective privi-
> lege ends where the public peril begins" (*Pacific Report-
> er,* 529 P.2d 553 (1975)) [Van Hoose and Kottler, 1977,
> pp. 87-88].

The case was heard four times at various levels and ultimately
settled out of court for an undisclosed sum of money.

What legal principles allowed the court to establish this
action, which would violate the patient's right to privacy as a
valid expression of due care? This decision rested on two principles, which constitute exceptions to the general principle that
one has no legal duty to control the behavior of others. The
first is the existence of a "special relationship." Central to establishing whether a special relationship exists are the elements
of control and of foreseeability of risk. The court reasoned that

a therapist has a special relationship with a patient because of his ability, in inpatient settings, to physically control a patient in accordance with a hospital's general charge to ensure the public welfare. However, since Poddar was in therapy on an outpatient basis, how was the duty derived? A case in Pennsylvania, *Greenberg* v. *Barbour,* 332 F. Supp. 745 (E.D. Pa. 1971), where a patient known to be violent was refused admittance to an emergency service and then assaulted someone, established that the duty could be predicated on the potential ability to control the patient. In outpatient therapy, that potential power is the power to commit. The question of foreseeability of risk was predicated on the idea that clinical psychologists and psychiatrists possess a special knowledge that enables them to predict dangerousness and hence make the risk foreseeable. One commentator (Olsen, 1977, p. 288), reviewing the research evidence on the ability to predict dangerousness, summarized it thus: "The consensus of opinion by responsible, scientific authorities is that the profession is incapable of accurately predicting the dangerousness of mental patients." Justice Stanley Mosk, in his opinion, addressed this point when he said that adherence to the concept of a standard of care (that degree of knowledge ordinarily possessed and exercised by therapists in similar conditions), when no skill exists, would "take us from the world of reality to the wonderland of clairvoyance." However, the majority of the court felt that such "knowledge" is being used every day: in child abuse cases, to determine whether parents are dangerous to their children; in commitment cases, to determine whether persons should be involuntarily committed to treatment institutions; and in criminal cases, to assess culpability and likelihood of further crime. According to the majority opinion, these practices imply some standard of knowledge—a standard determined by expert testimony; consequently, a breach of that standard can also be determined.

The second principle that generates a duty to control another's behavior is this: If one undertakes an affirmative action to reduce the risk that another person presents, and if that action increases the manifest risk, one is liable for his own actions and their consequences.

If you blow it & make it worse, you're responsible.

In the *Tarasoff* case, then, all the worst possible features involved in the principles underlying one's duty to control another's behavior converged. First, the therapist predicted violence, hence establishing a conviction that he held special knowledge. Second, this prediction was borne out, reinforcing the principle of foreseeability of risk through special knowledge. Third, the therapist made an active attempt to reduce the risk by committing Poddar, and that attempt was unsuccessful—in the court's eyes "bungled." Poddar then quit therapy, thereby creating a duty, on the part of the therapist, to avert the additional risk created by the disruption of the therapeutic relationship. These factors led the court to determine that, in this situation, a duty to warn was a valid expression of due care.

We are now entering the post-*Tarasoff* era. In two cases to date, judges have cited *Tarasoff* as a precedent in reaching their decision. In *McIntosh* v. *Milano,* 168 N.J. Super. 466 (1979), Lee Morgenstein, a patient of Dr. Milano's, murdered Kimberly McIntosh, a girl with whom he had once had had a relationship but who no longer wished to see him. Morgenstein had demonstrated his dangerousness by firing a gun at Kimberly's car, verbally threatening her and her dates, bringing a knife to a therapy session, and discussing fantasies of violent retribution. The plaintiff's experts contended that this behavior made Lee Morgenstein's dangerousness a known fact, not a prediction. The court held that a therapist "may have a duty to take whatever steps are reasonably necessary to protect an intended or potential victim of his patient when he determines, or should determine, in the appropriate factual setting and in accordance with the standards of his profession that the patient is or may present a probability of danger to that person." This hearing served to assert that a duty did exist and that there was a factual question to be presented to a jury, who would determine whether the duty was breached. In sum, *Tarasoff* was affirmed in New Jersey.

Interestingly, the court also noted that since a communicated threat to kill is a crime, and any person who fails to report a high misdemeanor is also guilty of a misdemeanor, the therapist's failure to inform the authorities might constitute a misdemeanor, in addition to negligence.

In the second case, *Shaw* v. *Glickman,* No. 1210 (Md. App. 1980), a Mr. Billian, his wife, and her lover, Dr. Shaw, were all in therapy with a treatment team led by Dr. Gallant. (Glickman was the personal representative of the estate of the late Dr. Gallant.) The husband caught the lovers in flagrante delicto and emptied a revolver into the man. The plaintiffs contended that Dr. Gallant was negligent because he failed to warn Dr. Shaw of the husband's "unstable and violent condition and the foreseeable and immediate danger that it presented to Dr. Shaw." The court determined that no intent to kill or injure was revealed to the therapist, so a duty to warn did not exist in this case. It also noted that the statutory privilege accorded patient-therapist communication should be respected except in "those instances where the privilege of confidentiality is expressly prohibited." Except for those express statutory waivers of privilege, the court declared, there is no justification for violating a patient's confidences; and, in fact, it would have been "a violation of the statute for Dr. Gallant or any member of his psychiatric team to disclose to Dr. Shaw any propensity on the part of Billian to invoke the old Solon law and shoot his wife's lover." The court declined to consider whether the creation of a duty to warn was in the public interest and chose merely to reaffirm the existing statute. In sum, *Tarasoff* was rejected in Maryland.

These two cases, resulting in diametrically opposed decisions, point to the unpredictability of the law. Unless a duty to warn is expressly determined in one's jurisdiction, a decision to warn or not to warn may make one the notorious precedent for that state. *Tarasoff* is being considered in these cases, but it is not being passively accepted by other states. It is this situation that points up the need for statutory remedies spelling out duties in advance whenever possible, rather than discovering them and applying them retroactively.

Irreducible Risks

A review of the commentaries on this case yields a table of risk situations for legal liability in the management of the dangerous patient. In this configuration, let us assume three possible situations (see Table 1). In the first situation, the ther-

Table 1. Risk Situations for Legal Liability

State of Therapist's Knowledge of Patient's Dangerousness	Actions by Therapist	Actions by Patient	Plaintiff	Likely Forms of Suit
Convinced	Unsuccessful commitment or a warning to intended victim	No violent act	Patient:	Negligent Diagnosis Defamation of Character Malicious Prosecution Invasion of Privacy
			Victim:	Negligent Diagnosis Infliction of Emotional Distress
Convinced (*Tarasoff* situation)	Unsuccessful commitment, no warning	Violent assault	Patient:	Negligent Diagnosis Negligent Care
			Victim:	Negligent Diagnosis Negligent Care
Should Have Known	No action	Violent assault	Patient:	Negligent Diagnosis Negligent Care
			Victim:	Negligent Diagnosis Negligent Care

apist is convinced of danger and has been unable to contain the situation within the therapeutic frame. He therefore decides to rupture the therapeutic frame and commit the patient or warn the victim. If he were successful, via commitment, in heading off violence, the patient would have a hard time proving that, given his freedom, he would not have hurt anyone. Also, if the warning averted a tragic outcome from an attempt, it would be seen as justified. However, when the therapist's commitment action is unsuccessful and the patient subsequently commits no violent act, or when the therapist warns the victim and, again, the patient commits no violent act, liability is likely to ensue. In the second situation, a description of the characteristics of the *Tarasoff* case, the therapist is convinced of danger; attempts to avert it by committing the patient but is unsuccessful in his commitment attempt; and fails to warn the victim. In this situation, liability is likely to ensue if the patient kills or injures the victim. The third situation is a should-have-known situation. If the therapist did not know of the risk but should have, and he did not act, liability might arise if the patient did act.

Predicting Dangerousness

In the light of *Tarasoff* and later cases, we can conclude that the most prudent course for the therapist is to take all discussions of violent intentions by the patient seriously, and to discuss them with the patient at some length. What things are useful to know? First, is there a history of violent behavior dangerous to others? Kozol (1975, p. 8) states an often-held conclusion: "No one can predict dangerous behavior in an individual with no history of dangerous acting out." Thus, questioning for a history of violence is significant. Kozol goes on to say:

> A critical question in the assessment of a violent patient is whether his violent behavior was largely "reactive"—directing more attention to the social psychology of violence-prone situations rather than to the psychopathology of violence-prone individuals—or was, instead, significantly linked to the individual's relatively greater predisposition toward violent behavior. For this reason, a major focus of the evaluation must be the circumstances and details of the actual assaultive behavior in question. This may well be the most valuable single source of information. . . . Of paramount importance is a meticulous description of the actual assault. The potential for violent assaultiveness is the core of our diagnostic problem, and the description of the aggressor in action is often the most valuable single source of information. The patient's version is compared with the victim's version. In many cases we interview the victim ourselves. Our most serious errors in diagnosis have been made when we ignored the details in the description of the assault.

Apart from this, there is very little published that claims

to be useful in the prediction of violent behavior, or that suggests guidelines of actions to take to improve our knowledge even one iota. What about psychological testing to assist in the decision? In a comprehensive review of the literature on that subject, Megargee (1970, p. 145) came to the following conclusion: "Thus far, no structured or projective test scale has been derived which, when used alone, will predict violence in the individual case in a satisfactory manner. Indeed, none has been developed which will adequately postdict, let alone predict, violent behavior."

Dynamically, particular attention should be paid to the patient's level of socialization and capacity to feel and express concern for others. Attention should also be paid to the patient's level of impulsiveness and capacity for self-control. Where independent clinical evidence suggests possible physiological dysfunction, a complete physical examination, and possibly a neurological examination, should be conducted in addition to the psychiatric and psychological evaluations. Any symptom or sign of physical or neurological dysfunction should be thoroughly explored.

In all situations, including those in which a clear psychiatric diagnosis can be made, predictions regarding future violent behavior must be considered as an independent variable.

Management of the Dangerous Patient

Once the issues of violence have emerged in the therapy process, and a history elicited to help assess the risks, what steps ought to be taken next? Since, according to the materiality rule of informed consent, the patient must be informed about foreseeable material risks involved in treatment, the therapist might inform the patient of the limits of confidentiality in the relationship. A disclosure of violent intent may lead to loss of liberty and privacy, which constitutes a material or significant risk to a reasonable person. "To fail to disclose these limits is to hold oneself open to liability under the materiality rule. In fact, the failure to disclose the limits of confidentiality in the face of a concomitant duty to disclose threats to third parties may be entrapment" (Bersoff, 1976, p. 271). In group, family, and couples therapy, while the therapist must retain confidentiality and may demand it of the patients, there is at this time no privilege in a court of law; hence, disclosures of violent intentions in these treatment modalities may be repeated in court. Clinically, such disclosures may help the therapist assess the severity of the risk. The risk would seem greater if a patient makes threats of violence even after he has been informed that the therapist may have to notify the authorities of such threats.

Since one must inform patients only of foreseeable risks, it seems unnecessary to tell all patients initially that discussions of violent impulses might lead to a breach of the confidentiality of the relationship. One ought to consider bringing it up immediately when the issue arises, but not as a matter of course to all patients. Many are not violent, have no history of violence, and no concerns about violence.

Roth and Meisel (1977) outline the following modifications of treatment that might be considered to retain the fabric of therapy and inform the potential victim.

1.   Ask the patient to warn the victim himself. (This has dangerous possibilities of a threatening confrontation escalating into the feared violence. The patient should be so informed.)
2.   Get a consent from the patient to warn the intended victim.
3.   Have a joint session with the patient and intended victim to disclose the threat and explore the factors leading up to it.
4.   Have the patient turn in any weapons he possesses.
5.   Increase the frequency of therapy sessions.
6.   Consider medication as an adjunct.
7.   Consider voluntary hospitalization.

Wexler (1979), viewing the *Tarasoff* decision in the light of victimological studies of violence, arrived at many of the same suggestions on how to manage the dangerous patient. He arrived at his conclusions on inviting the potential victim into the therapy for the following reasons:

1.   There is a high likelihood that the victims of violence occupy a significant relationship with their assailants.

2. Physical violence often is the end point of a history of re-
    ciprocally provocative behaviors, and it is merely a question
    of who will cross the barrier of restraint first.
3. The therapy may be enhanced by the new information that
    the potential victim has to share. (This echoes Kozol's find-
    ing that details of the violent acts, including interviews with
    the victim, are often the most useful information in pre-
    dicting future violence.)

The limitation of this perspective is that it requires an ongoing relationship between assailant and victim, each mutually
interested in resolving the conflicts in the relationship. This was
not so in the *Tarasoff* and *McIntosh* cases, where the relationships were over as far as the victims were concerned, but the assailants would not accept that fact.

These modifications help reduce the four negative effects
of warning a potential victim that the critics of the *Tarasoff* decision generally cite: (1) It will deter patients from therapy. (2)
It will inhibit their trust of the therapist. (3) It will inhibit frank
discussion of violent impulses and, by keeping them out of the
therapy situation, actually increase the risk. (4) It violates the
rights to privacy of the patient.

Throughout this process, it would be prudent to consult
with colleagues, particularly those with experience in treating
violent patients, and to document these consultations and one's
own deliberations over options and the reasons for all choices
made.

If the issue of dangerousness and the therapist's handling
of it leads to a precipitous, premature termination—so that the
therapy process no longer can be relied on to discharge one's
duty and, in the absence of therapy, a greater risk ensues—then
a duty to commit the patient or to warn the victim may arise.
Commitment is cited as having several advantages over a warning. Most notably, actual physical custody of the patient is the
most secure form of control possible. In addition, a possible
therapeutic process is still being attempted.

Critics of the duty to warn talk about the breach of trust
that it engenders and insist that it undermines the therapeutic

process. However, to institute commitment procedures is also often seen as a betrayal by the patient and one that is possibly felt more vividly as physical freedom is constrained. Just as the duty to warn might inhibit frankness and render the therapy impotent, so might a commitment lead the patient to be "good" and compliant in order to get a release rather than to try to work out the impulses therapeutically. I consider the real advantage of commitment to be solely the actual control of the patient. Vis-à-vis the duty to warn, it is a tradeoff of the loss of rights for the patient—liberty versus privacy.

There is a potential for abuse in this situation, in the form of a "defensive psychotherapy" that overcommits patients out of caution. As shown in Table 1, a commitment attempt that fails at this juncture exposes the therapist to the legal risk of suits for negligent diagnosis, defamation of character, invasion of privacy, and malicious prosecution, particularly if the patient then fails to carry out any threat. While the malicious prosecution would be hard to assert, the defense of truth to a defamation of character charge would be hard to assert because predictions of dangerousness are unreliable and because one cannot easily support an assertion that did not materialize.

If the commitment attempt is unsuccessful and the therapist is still convinced that the patient is dangerous or the patient does act out, the therapist faces the situation of the *Tarasoff* case. Roth and Meisel (1977, p. 509) accurately sum it up: "The paradox since *Tarasoff* is that the psychiatrist might need to give a warning to an identifiable potential victim because an unsuccessful commitment attempt may compromise treatment and increase the patient's potential for violence. This same patient may recently have been declared nondangerous by the court that refused to commit him." If the commitment is unsuccessful, the therapist must decide whether to risk liability for failing to warn if the patient does carry out the threat, or to risk liability for warning if nothing happens. At this point, the therapist may stand, as Roth and Meisel have pointed out, alone against the opinions of the court-appointed psychiatrists or psychologists and must fly in the face of a judicial decision of nondangerousness.

One must consider the possibility of suit by the patient (if he does harm to another and a warning was not given) that the therapist failed in his duty to control the patient and this failure led him to his own harm (jail). In a 1977 case in Iowa, reported by Dix (1981), Mary Cole, convicted of murdering her ex-husband, sued her psychiatrist for negligently failing to protect her from the consequences of her illness. In *Rosenfeld* v. *Coleman,* 19 Pa. D. & C. 2d 635 (1959), the principle was articulated that a therapist cannot actively engage in behavior that places the patient in legal jeopardy or even suggest illegal activities. Such actions may open the therapist to a charge of aiding and abetting a criminal offense. *Tarasoff* addresses passive failure to prevent a criminal act as a breach of duty to the patient and the third parties involved.

Once the decision to warn has been reached, many currently unanswered questions arise. Who is to be warned? What should one say? What are the liabilities to be faced from the victim?

Generally, it is suggested that the authorities and/or the intended victim should be warned. Warning the authorities makes the most sense when the intended victims are the patient's children, since a warning to the victim is ordinarily useless, and the child protective agency often has broader powers than the police—who might say that they cannot detain the patient (particularly after a failed commitment) because he has not done anything yet. If one decides to warn the victim—who is naturally shocked and terrified by the news that someone intends to kill him—and if nothing occurs, one could be liable for infliction of emotional duress by a negligent diagnosis. One way to reduce this risk might be to include as a part of the warning a statement of professional opinion about the nature and likelihood of the threat; to recommend that the victim contact the police, an attorney, and a mental health professional for assistance to detain (or try to commit) the patient; to inform the victim of his legal rights; and to offer assistance with the stress of such a situation. A warning to a victim incurs certain additional risks because that person is unknown to the therapist. The news given to a person of precarious emotional or physical health could lead to a heart attack, profound depression, a suicide attempt, or a panic attack.

Once the warning has been given, what options, after contacting the authorities, do victims have? They can arm themselves or hire bodyguards, or they can absent themselves, permanently or for a short time. Either course of action—for example, the loss of job due to prolonged absence—could constitute an injury from a negligent warning. Since many victims and assailants are well known to each other, the victim may respond with anger, seek out the patient, and contribute to a violent confrontation, possibly bringing harm to both that the warning was designed to avoid.

If a promise to warn has been made, failure to follow through with the promised action may result in a court action. In *Fair* v. *United States,* 234 F.2d 288 (5th Cir. 1956), a hospital had agreed to warn a nurse that a patient who had threatened to kill her had been released. The warning was not given, and he killed her and the two Burns security guards assigned to protect her. The estates of the nurse and the guards sued for negligence, and the trial court found for the plaintiffs.

Since many violent situations are domestic, known by police to be the most dangerous to third parties, there is also risk to the therapist's safety in a warning. An enraged, possibly paranoid male patient who intends to kill his wife may regard the therapist's warning, particularly if the therapist is male, as part of a joint conspiracy to unman him. As a result, the patient may add the therapist to his list of victims.

As these possibilities show, a warning can have undesirable consequences, which may contribute to legal liability. It may be the only avenue left, but it is a precarious path at best.

Certain important questions raised by the *Tarasoff* decision will have to be answered by future courts. For example, what forms of danger require a warning? Each state has certain statutory requirements for breaking confidentiality, and liability may ensue if the therapist fails to adhere to them. The therapist ought to be informed of the limits on confidentiality in his jurisdiction. What about the dangerousness of the suicidal or alcoholic airplane pilot whose negligence at his hazardous employment makes him dangerous? California has clearly declined to extend the duty to warn to suicide. In *Bellah* v. *Greenson,* 81 Cal. App. 3d 614 (1978), the parents of a patient who committed suicide sued the psychiatrist because he had not warned them about the patient's suicidal tendencies; the court ruled, however, that the *Tarasoff* decision is applicable only to cases of violent assault, not danger to property or self-inflicted harm. What about a duty to warn if one does not know who the victim is? Or if the threat is to a class of people, such as women or blacks? Finally, what if the patient admits to a violent crime that another person has wrongfully been convicted of? All such questions will need to be considered in the framework of one general question: What, if anything, can mental health professionals contribute to the prediction and control of the violent individual?

5

●●●●●●●●●●●●●●●●●●●●●●●●●●●●●●●

The
Suicidal
Patient

●●●●●●●●●●●●●●●●●●●●●●●●●●●●●●●●●

Therapists have an absolute duty to take steps to prevent suicide if they can reasonably anticipate the danger of self-destruction. Liability generally ensues in the management of the suicidal patient in two ways: (1) The therapist failed to act in a
way to prevent the suicide; in specific, the causes of action are
typically a *negligent diagnosis,* and concomitant failure to hospitalize, or *abandonment* by an inadequate response to an
"emergency" situation. (2) A therapist's act directly contributed to the suicide. Examples include a breach of confidence so
damaging as to lead to the suicide; negligent prescription of
medication in lethal quantities to a suicidal or depressed patient; clear directives for action that lead to a suicide; and, far
more subtly, the fostering of dependence in a patient to the extent that a suicidal crisis is precipitated when therapy is, or is
about to be, terminated. The key questions in the assessment of
liability are foreseeability and control. Did the therapist know
or should he have known of the foreseeable risk? Were adequate
attempts made to control the patient?

Foreseeability and Diagnosis

Since the first issue is foreseeability, an adequate diagnosis or attempt to diagnose is essential. Following are some areas worth exploring in the assessment of suicidal risk. They have been culled from the checklists developed by Slaby, Lieb, and Tancredi (1975) and by Tabachnick and Farberow (1961).

Demographic Indicators of Risk. The following indicators are especially noteworthy:

1. *Sex.* More women attempt suicide, but more men succeed.
2. *Age.* Suicide risk and age are positively correlated. Before age ten, suicide is rare. The rate rises steadily with age in men until thirty-five. The rate for women does not level off until seventy.
3. *Race.* On the whole, suicide risk is greater among whites than nonwhites; young black males, however, have a rate nearly twice that of young white males, and in urban centers the black rate approximates that of the white population.
4. *Ethnic origin.* Rates among foreign born tend to be higher than among native born, and the rates tend to be those of the person's country of origin.
5. *Family history.* Risk is increased if there is a family history of suicide, especially in the same-sex parent.
6. *Religion.* Suicide rates are lowest among Jews and Catholics. Protestants have significantly higher rates.
7. *Socioeconomic status.* The incidence of suicide is inversely related to socioeconomic class.
8. *Occupational and hobby choices.* If a person's occupation or hobbies have elements of significant danger and that danger is minimized, denied, or cited as the main reason for the pursuit of that activity, there may be elements of a self-destructive wish in the choice, particularly if the person courts the danger by poor preparation for the activity.
9. *Marital status.* Divorced and widowed individuals have rates four to five times those of married persons. The suicide rate for single persons is twice that of married per-

sons. Rates are lowest for married persons, especially if they have children.

10. *Sexual orientation.* Individuals with a predominantly homosexual orientation have a higher risk, especially if they are depressed, aging, or alcoholic.

Predisposing Individual Characteristics. The following personality characteristics are often associated with increased suicidal risk:

1. Manipulativeness of the suicidal ideation. The more aware the person is of the realistic implication of his behavior (that is, self-destruction), the more serious is the self-destructive potential. Conversely, the more the person is consciously aware of and focused on the effect of his activity on *other* persons, the more likely it is that his behavior represents a nonlethal kind of self-destructive activity.

2. *Mood.* Suicide risk increases with depressed mood, especially if it is associated with vegetative signs—that is, loss of appetite, loss of energy, and difficulty in falling asleep or staying asleep through the night (chronic or severe insomnia alone indicates an increased suicide risk)—or with anxiety, tension, or agitation.

3. *Quality of interpersonal relations.* Intense and unmet dependency needs darken the picture. The more isolated the person is, the more likely a significant self-destructive potentiality exists within him. Isolation is particularly ominous if the person is also impulsive and has few internal resources to cope with stress. His isolation means that he has few, if any, external resources to assist him in coping with difficult situations. The frenetic and unstable search for relationships of the borderline personality also carries increased suicidal risk. Such a person's impulsiveness and enraged intolerance for the inevitable imperfections of relationships make him a high suicide risk. If a person is not related to others in a reasonably satisfying manner, there is an increased risk of suicide.

4. *Impulse control and coping mechanisms.* The more impul-

sive a person is, the greater the possibility of self-destructive acts. The more limited or inadequate a person's capacities to cope with stress, the greater the risk. Alcohol or drug use as a means of coping with stress is particularly dangerous. The concomitant loss of impulse control and judgment increases the risk of suicide.

5. *Thought disorder.* Any psychotic process with the loss of reality contact increases the risk, since the realistic consequences of the behavior are not appreciated. This disturbance becomes even more serious when it is combined with depressed mood, hypochondriacal concerns that reach the delusional stage, or command hallucinations ordering the person to kill himself.

External Stressors. Table 2 shows the rating scale developed by Holmes and Rahe (1967) to indicate the degree of stress brought about by various serious changes in a person's life.

Table 2. Life Event Stresses

Rank	Life Event	Mean Value
1	Death of spouse	100
2	Divorce	73
3	Marital separation	65
4	Jail term	63
5	Death of close family member	63
6	Personal injury or illness	53
7	Marriage	47
8	Fired at work	47
9	Marital reconciliation	45
10	Retirement	45
11	Change in health of family member	44
12	Pregnancy	40
13	Sex difficulties	39
14	Gain of new family member	39
15	Business readjustment	39
16	Change in financial state	38
17	Death of close friend	37
18	Change to different line of work	36
19	Change in number of arguments with spouse	35
20	Mortgage over $10,000	31
21	Foreclosure of mortgage or loan	30
22	Change in responsibilities at work	29

Table 2. Life Event Stresses (Continued)

Rank	Life Event	Mean Value
23	Son or daughter leaving home	29
24	Trouble with in-laws	29
25	Outstanding personal achievement	28
26	Wife begin or stop work	26
27	Begin or end school	26
28	Change in living conditions	25
29	Revision of personal habits	24
30	Trouble with boss	23
31	Change in work hours or conditions	20
32	Change in residence	20
33	Change in schools	20
34	Change in recreation	19
35	Change in church activities	19
36	Change in social activities	18
37	Mortgage or loan less than $10,000	17
38	Change in sleeping habits (much more, much less, different time)	16
39	Change in number of family get-togethers	15
40	Change in eating habits	15
41	Vacation	13
42	Christmas	12
43	Minor violations of the law	11

Reprinted with permission from T. H. Holmes and R. N. Rahe, "The Social Readjustment Rating Scale," *Journal of Psychosomatic Research*, 1967, *11*, 213-218. Copyright 1967, Pergamon Press, Ltd.

The scale creates a range of "normal" evaluations of the magnitude of stress. The top item, "Death of Spouse," is arbitrarily set at a value of 100; then all other scores are a ratio of 100. If a particular person wants to kill himself over a change in social activities (number 36 on the scale), such a reaction—barring any extraordinary circumstances—seems unusually severe. The scale, then, helps to distinguish a "reasonably normal" person under a great deal of legitimate stress from a person who has very low tolerance for stress and poor coping mechanisms. It can be used to compare the magnitude of the person's reaction to the empirically derived magnitude of the stress. Obviously, the more points accrued, the greater the experienced stress, and the more reason for concern.

Methods of Attempt. Most people who ultimately commit

suicide have a history of at least one previous attempt. In decreasing order of lethality, the most common methods of suicide are (1) firearms and explosives, (2) jumping from high places, (3) cutting and piercing of vital organs, (4) hanging, (5) drowning (cannot swim), (6) poisoning (solids and liquids), (7) cutting and piercing of nonvital organs, (8) drowning (can swim), (9) poisoning (gases), (10) analgesic and soporific substances. In general, the more lethal the attempts have been, the greater the risk.

The more provisions made for rescue, the less lethal is the potentiality for self-destruction in any given attempt. This factor depends on the method used and the person's knowledge of the lethality of the method chosen (that is, the speed at which death occurs and the irreversibility of the damage). The more lethal the method, the greater the necessary planning to allow for rescue. If the person underestimates the lethality of the method chosen, he may make inadequate plans for rescue and die without intending to.

Management of the Suicidal Patient

When an assessment of foreseeable risk is made, the therapist must consider what management options to pursue. These prudent measures help to establish that a reasonable attempt to control the patient was made. The options are essentially the same as those for the dangerous patient:

1. Elicit from the patient, if possible and credible, a promise that he will control his impulses or will call the therapist or a local emergency service.
2. Make sure that any weapons in the patient's possession are placed in the hands of a third party.
3. Increase the frequency of therapy sessions.
4. Contact significant others in the patient's social network (with a consent) and ask them to assist in supporting the patient between sessions or in conjoint sessions.
5. Utilize a call-in system between sessions to monitor the patient's stability.

6. Consider using medication as an adjunct to the therapy. Bear in mind, however, that antidepressants may initially increase the risk, since the seriously depressed patient may become sufficiently energized to make an attempt; or a patient may hoard the medication until a lethal dose is collected and then used for a suicide attempt. (A table for deciding how much medication may be safely dispensed is presented in Chapter Six.)

7. Hospitalize the patient—either on a voluntary basis or, if necessary, through commitment.

Once a therapist determines that a significant risk exists, some action must be taken. The major areas of liability for an outpatient therapist when risk has been determined are failure to commit or hospitalize; inappropriate hospitalization (for instance, recommending an open-ward facility when a more secure facility is needed or, in contrast, recommending a highly restrictive facility when an open-ward facility would be sufficient); and failure to respond to a crisis, or abandonment.

The abandonment issue is probably the thorniest. It usually occurs when the therapist feels that the patient's threats and gestures are largely manipulative and reflect rage rather than despair. If he becomes intensely involved in rescuing the patient, the therapist reasons, he merely gratifies this risky, exhausting, and enraging mode of interpersonal transaction and only reinforces the pathology, rather than helping the patient give it up as a mode of being. How, then, can the therapist respond? That is, how can he preserve the patient's life while not merely completing the choreography of manipulation that the patient has begun?

Manipulative suicide threats raise a host of disturbing feelings: anxiety, as the therapist tries to assess the degree of risk and to respond therapeutically, always with insufficient information; guilt, if he does not respond as the patient demands, particularly if the threat is executed; anger at the interpersonal terrorism, the demand to cure under threat of a death that abuses our respect for life in the service of a narcissistic indulgence. Additionally disturbing is the possible lawsuit brought by the family of a suicide, alleging abandonment. In such a case, the therapist will be made to look like a callous, heartless person who abandoned a poor fellow human, drowning in his own sea of despair.

How does one protect oneself from liability incurred by an untoward result, yet not be held eternal hostage to these threats? First, a therapist may screen his patients and refuse to treat those who would present serious threats or who have a chronic history of suicidal threats and gestures. Second, if the therapist decides that a patient is merely manipulative, he must also decide how intensely the patient is willing to play. Some therapists, if convinced of the manipulative aspect but concerned about the patient's willingness to die, use an explicit contract that suicidal threats or gestures are the province of the local emergency service and that therapy will continue after the crisis is resolved but not during.

This raises the question of contracting away a duty of due care. The psychotherapist is in a different position than a physician, in that it is the unique relationship, not the replicable set of skills, that is the curative element, and an emergency service therapist will not be delivering the same care as the ongoing therapist. The issue is speculative and has not yet been tried in court. In any crisis where the therapist chooses not to respond, it may be prudent to refer the patient to an emergency service, so that, if an error in judgment regarding risk has been made, the patient is not limited only to the therapist as a support person.

Abandonment also can be charged any time the therapist fails to respond to a patient contact—usually because the therapist is on vacation or out of town for some other reason. The therapist should inform his patients of his absence, get their consent for him to share information necessary for coverage with the back-up therapist, and then pass on to that therapist whatever information is necessary for crisis management during the absence. He should mention, for example, complicating health factors, significant others as resources, prior episodes of violence or suicidal attempts, recent possible precipitating events, diagnostic information, and previously successful crisis strategies ("Keep him talking," "Don't ask questions," and so on).

The issue of appropriate referral can be stated as the conflict between the mandate to use the least restrictive alternative versus the risks of an "open-door" facility. At the very least, the referring therapist should be aware of the type of facility he is sending a patient to and should be sure that it is capable of providing the minimum level of restraint necessary to secure the safety of the patient. In addition, adequate information for a competent assessment and appropriately specific supervision orders need to be forwarded and made clear to all staff involved. Liability may ensue if a therapist withholds essential facts, gives negligent orders for supervision, or fails to make sure that his orders are correctly carried out.

If the therapist feels that close observation, restraint, and restriction would lead to an increase in feelings of rage, panic, and worthlessness, thereby increasing the risk of a suicide attempt, then an open-ward setting would seem to be appropriate. The mandate of a mental hospital is to be therapeutic, not merely custodial. If security precautions pose no obstacle to therapeutic gains, then it is reasonable to be secure. Custodial precautions do not stand entirely apart from treatment. They can indicate to the patient that the staff and the therapist understand him and care about him. Both too little and too much restraint may be grounds for liability—the former for malpractice, the latter for the abridgement of civil rights.

Benensohn and Resnik (1973) offer guidelines for "suicide proofing" a psychiatric unit. After discussions with hospitalized patients, they found that many of them do test out the physical layout of a ward and its adjoining areas. Taking into consideration that the most frequent methods of suicide in a hospital are hanging, jumping, cutting, and lethal ingestion, they make the following suggestions:

1. Count silverware and all other sharp objects before and after use by the patients.
2. Do not allow patients to spend much time alone in their rooms, and abolish private rooms altogether.

3. Jump- and hang-proof the bathrooms by installing break-away shower rods and recessed shower nozzles, and by removing exposed pipes and locating ventilation ducts at floor level.
4. Keep electric cords to a minimum length.
5. Install windows of unbreakable glass, with either tamper-proof screens or partitions too small to pass through. Keep all windows locked.
6. Lock all storage and utility rooms and adjacent stairwells, offices, or kitchens. Security precautions need to be impressed on all the nonclinical staff, including housekeepers and maintenance men.
7. Have visitors clear all gifts with staff first, and search patients (for drugs, sharp objects, cords, and other such items) after their return from passes. A pass may signify that the patient is getting better and now has enough energy to carry out a plan that the inertia of depression had previously made impossible.

Just as liability may ensue for failure to commit, or commitment without reasonable cause, so may it ensue for failure to release or for improper release. A comprehensive assessment of the patient's status should be made at the time of discharge planning, including the assessments of all staff who were involved with the patient and all entries in the patient's chart. The discharge summary ought to indicate the reasoning that supported the release and an assessment of the risk-benefit ratio. Ideally, the risk ought to be irreducibly low, with high benefit likely. The most difficult part of the decision probably lies in assessing how much of the patient's behavior was mere compliance to gain his freedom versus a true use of the program. This problem looms very large with committed patients.

Responsibility for Suicide

As noted at the beginning of this chapter, the therapist may be held liable either for failing to prevent a suicide or for directly causing the suicide. The second area of liability addresses the legal concept of proximate cause; that is, a plaintiff must show that the therapist's action, unbroken by any independent intervening actions, was sufficient to cause the suicide and that the suicide would not have occurred without this action.

Howell (1978), in a law review article, describes the current tests of responsibility used for assessing liability for suicide. Specifically, a therapist will be held liable (1) if his negligence created in the patient an *uncontrollable impulse* that led to suicide or (2) if his negligence was a *substantial factor* in creating a mental illness that led to suicide. The uncontrollable impulse doctrine means that a therapist's negligence must directly lead to an uncontrollable impulse in the patient to kill himself. Contributory negligence can be invoked against a patient if he was not entirely beyond reason. In five states (Iowa, Missouri, New Jersey, Oregon, and Vermont), the test for being "beyond reason" or in the grip of an "uncontrollable impulse" is the total absence of rational action or method in the suicide. The uncontrollable impulse doctrine is not the standard in every state and hence is not always applicable. The substantial factor doctrine is a step toward broadening the standard for therapist liability. An uncontrollable impulse is very hard to prove, especially if bizarre means of suicide are necessary to the proof. The law felt that an undue burden was placed on plaintiffs, and so a move was made to assign liability if a mental illness leading to suicide was created by therapist negligence—a broader standard than uncontrollable impulse. Also, the therapist's negligence needs to be only a substantial factor, not the sole factor—a further expansion of the basis of liability from the uncontrollable impulse test.

The substantial factor test may place an undue burden on the defendant, since an already unstable patient may regard a minor injury as a substantial reason for suicide. However, a therapist—by virtue of his special relationship to the patient—may be expected to be able to foresee the unreasonable or irrational response patterns of patients to external stimuli and so might be held liable by this test when defendants with other relationships to the patient would not.

Suicide, more dramatically than any other action, raises the question of contributory negligence on the patient's part. He dies by his own hand. Contributory negligence is a bar to recovery on a claim. However, the trend in the law is to move from the absolutist position of the contributory negligence doctrine to the relative one of comparative negligence, where relative fault is assigned to accord damages. Where contributory negligence is applied, it is not used when conditions placed the patient beyond the sphere of responsibility for his acts. When does that situation arise? Prosser (1964) says that the issue of the contributory negligence of the mentally disturbed person is a question of fact to be determined by a court *unless* the evidence discloses that the person whose acts are being judged is *completely* devoid of reason. Hence, as previously noted, one is beyond the sphere of responsibility only when one is completely devoid of reason. This contributory negligence may not be used with children, the mentally retarded, or those declared legally incompetent.

6

●●●●●●●●●●●●●●●●●●●●●●●●●●●●●●●●●

Psychotherapeutic Drugs and Electroconvulsive Therapy

●●●●●●●●●●●●●●●●●●●●●●●●●●●●●●●●●

Psychotherapeutic Drugs

There are two major approaches to legal liability for the use of psychotherapeutic medications. One is the intentional tort of assault and battery for the administration of a drug without consent, and the other is a malpractice action. The major risk areas giving rise to a lawsuit in this area are (1) failure to secure proper consent or to fully inform the patient of the proper way to use the medication; (2) negligent prescription—for example, wrong drug, wrong dosage, toxic combination of drugs; (3) failure to order or conduct a proper physical examination and to take a drug usage history prior to prescribing medication; (4) improper monitoring of medication, especially with the suicidal patient; and (5) the use of drugs as punishing agents in aversive therapy.

Informed Consent. Therapists must obtain informed consent for the use of all psychotherapeutic medications. To administer medication, such as prolixin by injection, without consent may leave one open to a battery charge.

The details of the elements of an informed consent and the circumstances under which it may be waived (that is, when therapeutic privilege can be exercised) are presented in Chapter Two. However, briefly, consent must be obtained voluntarily from a competent patient or his legal guardian. A full disclosure of certain aspects of the treatment must be made in simple, nontechnical language unless (1) the treatment is necessitated by an emergency; (2) full disclosure would cause the patient to reject, in the physician's opinion, a minimally risky medication; or (3) full disclosure would so disturb the patient's psychological balance as to create an added risk in the use of the medication. The physician should be prepared to explain to the patient the reasonable benefits to be expected by the use of the medication, the foreseeable material risks of the medication, the risks of no treatment, and the available alternatives to medication. The physician should know the following information about any medication prescribed: (1) side effects of the medication and how to control them; (2) the complications attendant to prolonged usage; (3) the signs indicating that the drug should be discontinued; (4) the adverse effects that may ensue from the combination of the prescribed drug with any other drugs, prescription or otherwise. If the therapist fails to give all this information to a patient, the therapist then is open to liability. He may be sued by the patient or by a third party who alleges that he was injured by the patient's actions and that these actions occurred because the physician had failed to disclose a potential risk to the patient.

The emergence of the tardive dyskinesia syndrome (the loss of bodily control) as a result of the use of psychotropic medications has made the question of consent loom ever larger. A terrible and possibly irreversible price can be extracted from patients for the benefits of controlling psychotic thought processes. The particular problem that tardive dyskinesia presents to the physician in eliciting an informed consent is that usually the medications that result in this syndrome are given to psychotic patients, and the conditions allowing therapeutic privilege usually are not present in these cases. First, a medical emergency does not exist unless command hallucinations of a destructive nature are present. Second, the risk we are discussing is certainly material, and a rejection could easily be the product of a rational cost-benefit decision (although the psychotic patient probably is incapable of making a rational decision). The third principle—that information about the dyskinesia may create additional anxiety in the patient, since loss of bodily control is a common fear of psychotics—is the only principle that would justify therapeutic privilege; and it requires the presence of concerns over bodily control on the part of the patient prior to the disclosure.

Halleck (1980) has suggested that, since the dyskinesia occurs only after prolonged use, one might not inform the patient of this risk, and only this risk, until psychotherapeutic effects are seen and the patient is in a position to weigh the benefits that the medication has to offer against the risk of tardive dyskinesia. Slovenko (1979), after a review of the literature, makes the following suggestions: (1) Information about tardive dyskinesia ought to be disclosed to the patient within three months of the administration of the medication, since the syndrome usually begins to appear after that period of time on medication. (2) The patient and family should be informed of early signs of the disorder, to aid in the detection process. (3) The therapist should administer the lowest doses possible to achieve acceptable levels of improvement. (4) Frequent drug-free holidays should be used, to attempt to unmask latent tardive dyskinesia—although, if such holidays last too long, a psychotic decompensation may be precipitated by the absence of the medication.

Finally, in our current medication-soaked society, a therapist may face liability if he fails to use a drug, or fails to refer the patient to a therapist who is competent to prescribe and monitor a drug known to be reasonably safe and effective for the patient's disorder or symptoms, or fails to inform the patient of a bias against using medication at all as an adjunct to verbal psychotherapy, so that the patient has no way of assessing when it might be useful to consider medication and make the decision to switch therapists or pursue medication independently.

Negligent Prescription. The negligent prescription of medication may take many forms. The wrong drug may be prescribed, or a pharmacist may prepare the wrong drug because the physician's handwritten prescription is illegible. The therapist may prescribe the wrong dosage or neglect to discontinue the medication despite the evidence of contraindicative signs. He may fail to assess a patient's condition by means of an adequate examination or interview or laboratory test. Or he may rely completely on the results of a laboratory test and ignore contradictory clinical evidence.

Despite the problems inherent in the administration of psychotherapeutic medications—most notably, the absence of clearly set dosages and the frequent necessity of using large amounts of medication to get any positive effect—there exists a powerful evidentiary tool in assessing the reasonableness of medication usage: the manufacturer's package insert regarding the drug's use. Although these printed instructions do not generally establish the standard of care, the more one deviates from them, the greater his potential risk. The Illinois Supreme Court in *Ohligschlager* v. *Proctor Community Hospital,* 55 Ill. 2d 411 (1973), decided that deviation from the package insert was prima facie evidence of negligence. A therapist who intends to use a new drug or to use an existing drug for a novel purpose would be wise to consider getting a Food and Drug Administration "investigational" clearance for the usage and, in every instance, should inform the patient of the drug's status.

As part of an adequate preparation to make a prescription, one should take a medical history, particularly to identify potential allergic reactions; a drug use history, to note effectiveness and length of time on certain medications, since that may affect the decision to continue with a medication or make a change; and, finally, a physical examination. These preliminary procedures are extremely important with the neuroleptic medications, where prolonged use can result in irreversible tardive dyskinesia. Exhibits 4 and 5 illustrate the type of medical his-

Exhibit 4. Medical History Form

Date _____

Name _____

Age _____

Family Physician _____

    Phone Number _____

Date and results of last physical examination. _____

_____

_____

Are you under current treatment for any health problems? If so, specify problem and treatment. _____

_____

Have you ever had any of the following difficulties? If so, indicate when, treatment received, and current status.

Allergies _____

Breathing Problems _____

Cancer/Tumor _____

Diabetes _____

Dizziness/Fainting _____

Seizures/Convulsions _____

Gland Problems _____

Back or Bone Injuries _____

Heart Disease/Stroke _____

High Blood Pressure _____

Ulcer/Stomach Problems _____

Headaches _____

Sleeping Problems _____

Surgery _____

Other Hospitalizations _____

tory form and drug usage profile that therapists, both medical and nonmedical, might use as part of an intake form. Forms such as these ought to be part of all intake processes, to identify patients with complicating health problems before treatment is enjoined. For example, one might not wish to treat a patient with a cardiac condition in a confrontational anxiety-provoking marathon group. These forms should be the starting point for a discussion of the patient's health, as it pertains to amenability for treatment and diagnosis, not the end of the process.

    Many psychiatrists, for a variety of reasons (chiefly because of the significant input that form of contact could have

Exhibit 5. Medication History

Name:_____ Age:_____ Date:_____

	Name of Drug	Fre-quency of Use	Dosage	Dates of Use		Allergic/ Idiosyncrat-ic Reaction (Specify)
				Start	End	
Antipsychotics*						
Antidepressants						
Anticholinergics						
Minor Tranquilizers/Barbiturates						
Other Prescribed Medication						
Over-the-Counter Medications						
Opiates						
Stimulants						
Marijuana/Hallucinogenics						
Alcohol						

*Request complete life history of use, to assess risk of tardive dyskinesia.

on the therapeutic relationship), do not give physical examinations to their patients on medication. However, the failure to conduct an examination prior to prescribing drugs is generally considered unacceptable medical practice; and, should an injury evolve, it is likely that expert witnesses would establish that an examination would have been the standard of care. If the therapist does not wish to conduct the examination himself, he would be well advised to refer the patient to an internist prior to prescribing the medication.

Medication and the Suicidal Patient. In monitoring the medication of the suicidal patient in an outpatient setting—where the patient is allowed to purchase or hoard a lethal dosage of medication and then uses it to attempt suicide—the therapist may be charged with failing to appreciate the suicidal risk of the patient (see Chapter Five for detailed exposition of the risks and avenues of management) or failing to take reasonable steps to control the medication the patient is receiving.

Brophy (1967) devised tables of guidelines for the reasonably safe dosages of many commonly used psychotherapeutic drugs. He assumed a healthy adult, free of idiosyncratic responses, and then devised two measures: the Average Daily Dose (ADD), based on the insert; and the Massive Dose (MD), based on literature reports. The ratio of ADD:MD represents the supply, in number of days, that constitutes a predictably massive or potentially lethal dose to a healthy adult. The Average Weekly Dose (AWD) is also listed for convenience in looking up medications by their typically dispensed weekly amounts.

As Table 3 shows, the drugs break down into two groups: those safe at the greater than 1:30 ratio—namely, the major and minor tranquilizers, with the exception of meprobamate; and those safe in ratios of less than 1:15, meprobamate and the antidepressants. Unfortunately, the drugs most given to suicidal patients—the antidepressants—are the very drugs that are considered safe *only* in supplies of less than two weeks.

Once a reasonable amount can be decided on for the prescription, the problem of the patient's hoarding the medication to accrue a massive dose must be dealt with. If a responsible family member can be found to help the patient throw away

Table 3. Lethal Dosages of Common Psychotherapeutic Drugs

Major Tranquilizers

Generic Name	Trade Name	ADD	AWD	MD	Largest Ingestion with Recovery	ADD:MD Ratio
Chlorpromazine	Thorazine	100 mg	700 mg	6,000 mg	30,000 mg	1:60
Thioridazine	Mellaril	75 mg	545 mg	2,500 mg	20,000 mg	1:30
Chlorprothixene	Taractan	50 mg	350 mg	2,500 mg	8,000 mg	1:50
Perphenazine	Trilafon	16 mg	110 mg	500 mg	—	1:40
Trifluoperazine	Stelazine	8 mg	60 mg	500 mg	—	1:60

Minor Tranquilizers

Generic Name	Trade Name	ADD	AWD	MD	Largest Ingestion with Recovery	ADD:MD Ratio
Chlordiazepoxide	Librium	30 mg	210 mg	1,000 mg	2,225 mg	1:30
Diazepam	Valium	15 mg	105 mg	700 mg	—	1:50
Meprobamate	Equanil	1,200 mg	8,400 mg	8,000 mg	38,400 mg	1:7
Oxazepam	Serax	45 mg	315 mg	1,000 mg	—	1:25

Antidepressants

Generic Name	Trade Name	ADD	AWD	MD	Largest Ingestion with Recovery	ADD:MD Ratio
Tricyclics						
Amitriptyline	Elavil	100 mg	700 mg	1,000 mg	4,700 mg	1:10
Desipramine	Norpramine	100 mg	700 mg	1,000 mg	2,500 mg	1:10
Imipramine	Tofranil	100 mg	700 mg	1,200 mg	5,375 mg	1:12
Nortriptyline	Aventyl	60 mg	420 mg	1,000 mg	2,100 mg	1:15
MAOI						
Isocarboxazid	Murplan	20 mg	140 mg	250 mg	500 mg	1:12
Nialamide	Niamid	75 mg	525 mg	900 mg	—	1:12
Pheneizine		45 mg	315 mg	525 mg	750 mg	1:10
Tranylcypromine	Parnate	20 mg	140 mg	250 mg	750 mg	1:12

Source: J. J. Brophy, "Suicide Attempts with Psychotherapeutic Drugs," Archives of General Psychiatry, 1967, 17, 652-657. Copyright 1967, American Medical Association.

unnecessary and dangerous medications, and to dispense the prescribed medication to the patient and observe him taking it, the problem can be fairly easily dealt with. Otherwise, cumbersome plans must be made for the therapist to personally monitor the taking of the medication, even on a daily basis.

Drugs as Aversive Therapy. The use of drugs as punishing agents in aversive therapy—for example, Antabuse in the management of alcoholics—leaves one open, in addition to the malpractice and battery actions, to actions based on constitutional law, such as cruel and unusual punishment. In these cases, a fully informed consent is essential. In addition, the therapist might do well to use a noxious treatment agent *only* as the final treatment approach, after the less noxious treatment approaches have been exhausted.

Psychotherapeutic medications once held great promise as the "wonder drugs" to cure mental illness. Their use strikes right at the heart of major questions in the understanding of mental illness. Is the behavior to be changed the problem itself or just a symptom? Do the drugs cure or merely mask the existence of disturbed mental processes? There are important social aspects to this question when medication is forced on individuals or used for strictly aversive ends. Many contend that the medication approach to problems in human living is a problem in itself, a form of institutionalized prescribed addiction to calm people down, not help them discover their own personal resources. There has been a push by psychiatry to review the interest in medication as the treatment of choice. Excessive medication may be seen as pacification of the client, not treatment. At the same time, the failure to consider medication may be regarded as neglect of a patient. The decision whether or not to use medication in the future has all the hallmarks of public policy considerations that tort actions aim to address: Are drugs being used for control purposes or for therapy purposes? Does society wish to take a stand on who will control—and why and how?

Electroconvulsive Therapy

Electroconvulsive therapy has been in use long enough and is close enough in type to other medical treatments, in its replicability with known risks, that the guidelines for negligence are clearer than in almost any other area of psychotherapeutic practice. In fact, it is probably the only treatment modality where an attempt has been made to publish guidelines of practice that represent that elusive "standard of care." The major areas of risk are (1) inappropriate patient—one with a preexisting physical condition or inappropriate psychopathological symptoms; (2) failure to obtain a proper informed consent; (3) negligent care in preparing the patient for electroconvulsive therapy; (4) injury caused by the electroconvulsive therapy; (5) negligence in posttherapy care; and (6) electroshock used as aversive therapy.

Patient Choice. Since the major injuries that can result from electroconvulsive therapy are broken bones and cardiac arrhythmias, any patient with a preexisting orthopedic condition, such as osteoporosis (as was the case in *Collins* v. *Hand,* 431 Pa. 378 (1968)), or a history of cardiac arrhythmia might be considered an inappropriately risky patient for this treatment. In the *Collins* case, the patient had osteoporosis and during electroconvulsive therapy suffered broken acetabula. She charged the physician with negligence because he had failed to read X-rays that would have informed him of her condition. (In this case the Pennsylvania State Supreme Court found for the defendant.)

Electroconvulsive therapy has been used most frequently and successfully with depressed patients. In fact, Schwitzgebel and Schwitzgebel (1980, p. 95) summarize its efficacy as "75-90 percent effective in removing depressive symptomatology of involutional melancholia and persistent endogenous depression of middle-aged and older patients unresponsive to several months of treatment with psychotherapy and drugs."

Because of its documented efficiency, it is conceivable that the therapist who failed to consider it as a treatment alternative, or failed to obtain a consultation to consider its use, might face a suit for negligent care. This is a very sensitive area because a decision by a court would amount to the court's creating an affirmative duty to provide a specific treatment, thus moving into the area of medical judgment.

Electroconvulsive therapy is not a documentedly successful or common treatment for symptomatology other than depression. To use electroconvulsive therapy for treatment of anxiety symptoms, for example, might leave one open to a suit for negligent or inappropriate treatment.

Insulin and Metrazol Coma Therapy was devised for the purpose of treating basic anxiety; however, it is rarely used now because of the relatively high death rate (ten times the death rate associated with electroconvulsive therapy); the risk of prolonged coma, leading to brain damage; or the failure to restore normal brain functioning after the sugar is administered.

Obviously, one must first make an accurate diagnosis of the patient and to do a sufficient history taking and examination to rule out those physically ill suited for this treatment.

Informed Consent. The second major area of risk is the obtaining of an informed consent. As spelled out in Chapter Two, an informed consent should be obtained voluntarily from a competent individual or the individual's legal guardian. The person should be told of his right to refuse treatment, the benefits and risks of the treatment, the risks of no treatment, and the alternatives available to electroconvulsive therapy. The consent should be written and signed, probably at the time of the initial treatment.

Again, a therapist need not obtain a fully informed consent in the following situations: (1) if it is an emergency; (2) if the knowledge imparted would cause a patient to forgo a necessary and minimally risky therapy; (3) if the knowledge imparted would so disturb the patient as to increase the risk of the treatment—for example, generating an anxiety state leading to an increased risk of cardiac arrhythmias.

The second situation is unlikely to occur, since electroconvulsive therapy clearly is not a minimally risky therapy. Beresford (1971, p. 101), in reviewing reports of several thousand electroconvulsive therapy treatments from 1964 to 1968, reported the following injuries: thirty-five vertebral fractures; thirteen cardiac arrhythmias, resulting in three deaths; seven slight burns; four deaths, causes known; one to two each dislocated shoulders, mandibles, broken teeth, and aspirational pneumonias. When the therapist advises the patient of the risks of electroconvulsive therapy, Beresford (1972, p. 129) suggests that the following hazards, at a minimum, be mentioned: "fractures, a postconvulsive disturbance in memory and orientation which is usually transient, and a small but definite risk of cardiorespiratory distress related to anesthesia."

Because of the postconvulsive memory disturbance, an unusual situation can occur where the patient, after a series of electroshocks has begun, will be unable to remember giving consent to the therapy and demand that it be stopped. The right to consent to a treatment is revokable at any time; however, the therapist must then decide whether the revocation is the product of a clear, rational mind or of the amnesia produced by the treatment. The therapist also needs to decide whether prematurely discontinuing the treatment would be detrimental to the health or life of the patient.

Preparation for Electroconvulsive Therapy. It is now standard practice to administer muscle relaxants and anesthetics to reduce the risk of fractures. However, the anesthetics carry the risk of depressing respiratory and cardiovascular functioning. Although relatively rare, this is potentially far more dangerous than the common fractures the anesthetics hope to avoid.

Because of this known risk, personnel and equipment necessary to deal with a cardiorespiratory emergency ought to be on hand.

Posttherapy Care. Because of the orientation and memory loss, patients need to be kept under close supervision so as not to get lost, fall, or injure themselves. The failure to provide adequate supervision might leave one open to a suit if an accident occurs. The administering physician should conduct a posttherapy examination of the patient for fractures or burns. The failure to do so and thus not diagnose or treat a therapy-caused injury leaves one open to a potential suit.

After the treatments have been terminated, the physician should inform the family members that during the convalescent period—a period of several weeks' duration following discharge from the hospital—the patient must be under strict supervision of some member of the family or some responsible person selected by the family. This precaution is necessary because of the temporary mental confusion and impairment of memory. During this entire period, the patient should not be permitted to drive an automobile, to transact any business, or to carry on his usual employment until the doctor gives his permission. He should not be permitted to leave the house unless accompanied by a responsible companion, because he may wander off and get lost. Supervision is very important and must be provided by a responsible person. Should an injury occur to a patient because the family was not informed of the posttreatment risks, there exists the definite possibility of a negligence suit.

Electroshock as Aversive Therapy. Nonconvulsive shock therapy is often used as part of an aversive conditioning program with autistic, retarded, or self-mutilating children. As with any intrusive therapy, a fully informed consent should be obtained. Moreover, the treatment should be considered only as a last resort form of therapy if all else fails, and it should be promptly discontinued if ineffective. Concurrently, a positive behavioral program should be instituted to help shape wanted behaviors and get the shock treatment discontinued as soon as possible.

7

●●●●●●●●●●●●●●●●●●●●●●●●●●●●●●●●

Effects of the Malpractice Crisis on Practice

Some Recommendations

●●●●●●●●●●●●●●●●●●●●●●●●●●●●●●●●

Having surveyed the literature and cases of the past, what can we expect to see emerging as legal trends in the 1980s, and how can the professions that practice psychotherapy respond to these trends?

My impression is that the law is not generally accomplishing its aims through judicial regulation of therapeutic practice. Torts aim to address public policy concerns in their decisions, but only the *Tarasoff* case has achieved profession-wide awareness. Other cases disappear without ripples, leaving similar cases to be tried again over and over in the same jurisdictions without generally affecting the practice of psychotherapy. Constitutional law cases, since they represent the laws of the land, do have greater impact on practice; however, they address only a small portion of the people who practice psychotherapy; namely, those who work with incarcerated or involuntarily committed patients. There have been divergent trends in recent tort and constitutional law that I feel work against increasing the quality of care patients receive. Tort law seems to be expanding our responsibility to control our patients, witness *Tarasoff,* while constitutional laws that make it ever more difficult to hospitalize patients make it also more difficult to execute that responsibility. The result is that while overcommitment is discouraged, high-risk patients—the ones potentially dangerous to themselves or others—are not being seen by many therapists, who do not wish to expose themselves to what they feel is an unacceptably risky situation.

I believe that legal liability for psychotherapy in the 1980s will change from past trends, partly because of changes in psychotherapeutic practice. The trends I foresee include the following:

1. Plaintiffs will make more use of intentional torts and contract law, to avoid the pitfalls of proximate cause and standard of care that are the downfall of so many malpractice actions.
2. An increased number of suits will be filed against public agency personnel as sovereign immunity is whittled away.
3. Increased use will be made of the informed consent doctrine in negligence cases, especially with verbal psychotherapies and with the potentially noxious effects of the cathartic therapies.
4. Malpractice suits will be more effective with the directive/behavioral therapies because of the relative ease of establishing proximate cause.
5. Undue influence suits will increase as a result of the increase in psychotherapy with the elderly.
6. Family therapy will generate suits by family members dissatisfied with outcomes. The balancing of rights and prerogatives is a task that the law is finding very difficult. Approaches that focus solely on the family as unit or system

of concern and lose sight of the inalienable rights of each and every individual may expose themselves to greater degrees of risk than other approaches.

7. Suits will be initiated because therapy has not been prompt enough in achieving its effects. The advent of short-term therapy makes the treatment decision not to use that approach a particularly risky one.

8. Insurance peer review actions may prompt suits. If a claim is rejected because the treatment plan was found to be inadequate, this may spark an action by a patient to recover the fees that he has paid for services.

9. Product liability suits will probably increase with the increased use of electroshock machines and biofeedback machines.

In response to these trends as I see them, the professions that practice psychotherapy might consider the following actions:

1. Therapists should support therapy outcome research (research that aims to specify treatment X practitioner X problem outcomes), so that treatment plans represent empirical knowledge, not merely the self-interest and ideology of competing sects. The existence of a deterioration effect in therapy can no longer be ignored and also ought to be fully researched.

2. Therapists should attempt to create reasonable expectations for the public about what psychotherapy can and cannot do. Perhaps a return to Freud's goals of ordinary human misery is called for, rather than our current pursuit of wrinkle-free, drip-dry, perfectible man.

3. If a therapy approach is innovative, perhaps it ought to be required to undergo federal research testing prior to general use with the public.

4. Currently there are almost no substantive standards of care for the delivery of psychotherapeutic care promulgated by any national professional organizations. While I envision the creation of such standards to be a dynamic process feeding into and shaped by sophisticated research, I do not believe we operate in a consensual vacuum, as this absence seems to indicate.

First steps need to be taken by the professions, or surely the law will do it for us.

5. The professions ought to address current laws on mental health at the state and national levels. For example, they should attempt to get privilege statutes rewritten to include group and family therapy and to create standards whereby confidentiality may be breached (an example would be the statutory immunity from liability for child abuse reports enacted by Virginia) without liability. In general, they should attempt to get the law to function as adviser and not solely as adversary after the fact.

6. Training in graduate school and continuing education for licensed practitioners ought to include legal education. Psychotherapy's step into the legal limelight, no matter how unwelcome, is an irrevocable one and cannot be ignored in training psychotherapists. Graduate school training (perhaps at the internship field placement or residency level) ought to include some work on the clinical difficulties in the assessment and treatment of the high-risk patient. Perhaps licensed practitioners ought to use some of their required continuing education credits to keep abreast of legal changes that affect their practice. Workshops for this purpose might be provided by the state boards that license psychotherapists.

Resources

●●●●●●●●●●●●●●●●●●●●●●●●●●●●●●●●●●●

Reproduced here are the following documents: (1) the National Association of Social Workers' *Code of Ethics* and (2) *Standards for the Private Practice of Clinical Social Work*; (3) the American Association for Marriage and Family Therapy's *Code of Professional Ethics*; (4) the American Psychiatric Association's *Principles of Medical Ethics, with Annotations Especially Applicable to Psychiatry,* and (5) "Recommendations Regarding the Use of Electroconvulsive Therapy," from the *Report of the Task Force on Electroconvulsive Therapy*; (6) the American Psychological Association's *Ethical Principles of Psychologists* and (7) *Specialty Guidelines for the Delivery of Services by Clinical Psychologists.*

Except where self-evident, cue words in the margins of these documents locate passages in the ethical or professional standards that relate to the concepts presented in this book. For example, the section on confidentiality and its limits in the *Ethical Principles of Psychologists* might be cued by the phrase "duty to warn."

These documents have been chosen because they are the policy statements of the national professional organizations that represent psychotherapists and, as such, are the closest things extant to recognized "standards of care." Although they are not legal standards, they are presented here to stimulate thought about one's professional practice.

97

A

●●●●●●●●●●●●●●●●●●●●●●●●●●●●●●●●●●●

National Association of Social Workers, Code of Ethics

I. The Social Worker's Conduct and Comportment as a Social Worker

  A. Propriety—The social worker should maintain high standards of personal conduct in the capacity or identity as social worker.

    1. The private conduct of the social worker is a personal matter to the same degree as is any other person's, except when such conduct compromises the fulfillment of professional responsibilities.

Fraud

    2. The social worker should not participate in, condone, or be associated with dishonesty, fraud, deceit, or misrepresentation.

    3. The social worker should distinguish clearly between statements and actions made as a private individual and as a representative of the social work profession or an organization or group.

  B. Competence and Professional Development—The social worker should strive to become and remain proficient in professional practice and the performance of professional functions.

    1. The social worker should accept responsibility or employment only on the basis of existing competence or the intention to acquire the necessary competence.

Fraud

    2. The social worker should not misrepresent professional qualifications, education, experience, or affiliations.

National Association of Social Workers, *Code of Ethics* (Washington, D.C.: National Association of Social Workers, 1979).

98

C. Service—The social worker should regard as primary the service obligation of the social work profession.

1. The social worker should retain ultimate responsibility for the quality and extent of the service that individual assumes, assigns, or performs.

2. The social worker should act to prevent practices that are inhumane or discriminatory against any person or group of persons.

D. Integrity—The social worker should act in accordance with the highest standards of professional integrity and impartiality.

1. The social worker should be alert to and resist the influences and pressures that interfere with the exercise of professional discretion and impartial judgment required for the performance of professional functions.

2. The social worker should not exploit professional relationships for personal gain.

Undue Influence

E. Scholarship and Research—The social worker engaged in study and research should be guided by the conventions of scholarly inquiry.

1. The social worker engaged in research should consider carefully its possible consequences for human beings.

2. The social worker engaged in research should ascertain that the consent of participants in the research is voluntary and informed, without any implied deprivation or penalty for refusal to participate, and with due regard for participants' privacy and dignity.

3. The social worker engaged in research should protect participants from unwarranted physical or mental discomfort, distress, harm, danger, or deprivation.

4. The social worker who engages in the evaluation of services or cases should discuss them only for the professional purposes and only with persons directly and professionally concerned with them.

5. Information obtained about participants in research should be treated as confidential.

6. The social worker should take credit only for work actually done in connection with scholarly and re-

search endeavors and credit contributions made by others.

II. The Social Worker's Ethical Responsibility to Clients

F. Primacy of Clients' Interests—The social worker's primary responsibility is to clients.

1. The social worker should serve clients with devotion, loyalty, determination, and the maximum application of professional skill and competence.

Undue
Influence

2. The social worker should not exploit relationships with clients for personal advantage, or solicit the clients of one's agency for private practice.

3. The social worker should not practice, condone, facilitate, or collaborate with any form of discrimination on the basis of race, color, sex, sexual orientation, age, religion, national origin, marital status, political belief, mental or physical handicap, or any other preference or personal characteristic, condition, or status.

Fiduciary
Duty

4. The social worker should avoid relationships or commitments that conflict with the interests of clients.

Sex as Innovative Therapy

5. The social worker should under no circumstances engage in sexual activities with clients.

6. The social worker should provide clients with accurate and complete information regarding the extent and nature of the services available to them.

Informed
Consent

7. The social worker should apprise clients of their risks, rights, opportunities, and obligations associated with social service to them.

Duty to
Consult

8. The social worker should seek advice and counsel of colleagues and supervisors whenever such consultation is in the best interest of clients.

Termination

9. The social worker should terminate service to clients, and professional relationships with them, when such service and relationships are no longer required or no longer serve the clients' needs or interests.

Abandonment

10. The social worker should withdraw services precipitously only under unusual circumstances, giving careful consideration to all factors in the situation and taking care to minimize possible adverse effects.

11. The social worker who anticipates the termination or interruption of service to clients should notify clients promptly and seek the transfer, referral, or continuation of services in relation to the clients' needs and preferences. Abandonment

G. Rights and Prerogatives of Clients—The social worker should make every effort to foster maximum self-determination on the part of clients.

1. When the social worker must act on behalf of a client who has been adjudged legally incompetent, the social worker should safeguard the interests and rights of that client.

2. When another individual has been legally authorized to act in behalf of a client, the social worker should deal with that person always with the client's best interest in mind.

3. The social worker should not engage in any action that violates or diminishes the civil or legal rights of clients.

H. Confidentiality and Privacy—The social worker should respect the privacy of clients and hold in confidence all information obtained in the course of professional service.

1. The social worker should share with others confidences revealed by clients, without their consent, only for compelling professional reasons.

2. The social worker should inform clients fully about the limits of confidentiality in a given situation, the purposes for which information is obtained, and how it may be used. Informed Consent

3. The social worker should afford clients reasonable access to any official social work records concerning them.

4. When providing clients with access to records, the social worker should take due care to protect the confidences of others contained in those records.

5. The social worker should obtain informed consent of clients before taping, recording, or permitting third party observation of their activities.

I. Fees—When setting fees, the social worker should ensure that they are fair, reasonable, considerate, and commensurate with the service performed and with due regard for the clients' ability to pay.

   1. The social worker should not divide a fee or accept or give anything of value for receiving or making a referral.

III. The Social Worker's Ethical Responsibility to Colleagues

J. Respect, Fairness, and Courtesy—The social worker should treat colleagues with respect, courtesy, fairness, and good faith.

   1. The social worker should cooperate with colleagues to promote professional interests and concerns.

   2. The social worker should respect confidences shared by colleagues in the course of their professional relationships and transactions.

   3. The social worker should create and maintain conditions of practice that facilitate ethical and competent professional performance by colleagues.

   4. The social worker should treat with respect, and represent accurately and fairly, the qualifications, views, and findings of colleagues and use appropriate channels to express judgments on these matters.

   5. The social worker who replaces or is replaced by a colleague in professional practice should act with consideration for the interest, character, and reputation of that colleague.

   6. The social worker should not exploit a dispute between a colleague and employers to obtain a position or otherwise advance the social worker's interest.

   7. The social worker should seek arbitration or mediation resolution for compelling professional reasons.

   8. The social worker should extend to colleagues of other professions the same respect and cooperation that is extended to social work colleagues.

   9. The social worker who serves as an employer, supervisor, or mentor to colleagues should make orderly

and explicit arrangements regarding the conditions of their continuing professional relationship.

10. The social worker who has the responsibility for employing and evaluating the performance of other staff members should fulfill such responsibility in a fair, considerate, and equitable manner, on the basis of clearly enunciated criteria.

11. The social worker who has the responsibility for evaluating the performance of employees, supervisees, or students should share evaluations with them.

K. Dealing with Colleagues' Clients—The social worker has the responsibility to relate to the clients of colleagues with full professional consideration.

1. The social worker should not solicit the clients of colleagues.

2. The social worker should not assume professional responsibility for the clients of another agency or a colleague without appropriate communication with that agency or colleague.

3. The social worker who serves the clients of colleagues, during a temporary absence or emergency, should serve those clients with the same consideration as that afforded any client.

IV. The Social Worker's Ethical Responsibility to Employers and Employing Organizations

L. Commitments to Employing Organization—The social worker should adhere to commitments made to the employing organization.

1. The social worker should work to improve the employing agency's policies and procedures, and the efficiency and effectiveness of its services.

2. The social worker should not accept employment or arrange student field placements in an organization which is currently under public sanction by NASW for violating personnel standards, or imposing limitations on or penalties for professional actions on behalf of clients.

    3. The social worker should act to prevent and eliminate discrimination in the employing organization's work assignments and in its employment policies and practices.

    4. The social worker should use with scrupulous regard, and only for the purpose for which they are intended, the resources of the employing organization.

V. The Social Worker's Ethical Responsibility to the Social Work Profession

    M. Maintaining the Integrity of the Profession—The social worker should uphold and advance the values, ethics, knowledge, and mission of the profession.

      1. The social worker should protect and enhance the dignity and integrity of the profession and should be responsible and vigorous in discussion and criticism of the profession.

      2. The social worker should take action through appropriate channels against unethical conduct by any other member of the profession.

      3. The social worker should act to prevent the unauthorized and unqualified practice of social work.

Fraud   4. The social worker should make no misrepresentation in advertising as to qualifications, competence, service, or results to be achieved.

    N. Community Service—The social worker should assist the profession in making social services available to the general public.

      1. The social worker should contribute time and professional expertise to activities that promote respect for the utility, the integrity, and the competence of the social work profession.

      2. The social worker should support the formulation, development, enactment, and implementation of social policies of concern to the profession.

    O. Development of Knowledge—The social worker should take responsibility for identifying, developing, and fully utilizing knowledge for professional practice.

1. The social worker should base practice upon recognized knowledge relevant to social work.
2. The social worker should critically examine and keep current with emerging knowledge relevant to social work.
3. The social worker should contribute to the knowledge base of social work and share research knowledge and practice wisdom with colleagues.

VI. The Social Worker's Ethical Responsibility to Society
   P. Promoting the General Welfare—The social worker should promote the general welfare of society.
   1. The social worker should act to prevent and eliminate discrimination against any person or group on the basis of race, color, sex, sexual orientation, age, religion, national origin, marital status, political belief, mental or physical handicap, or any other preference or personal characteristic, condition, or status.
   2. The social worker should act to ensure that all persons have access to the resources, services, and opportunities which they require.
   3. The social worker should act to expand choice and opportunity for all persons, with special regard for disadvantaged or oppressed groups and persons.
   4. The social worker should promote conditions that encourage respect for the diversity of cultures which constitute American society.
   5. The social worker should provide appropriate professional services in public emergencies.
   6. The social worker should advocate changes in policy and legislation to improve social conditions and to promote social justice.
   7. The social worker should encourage informed participation by the public in shaping social policies and institutions.

B

●●●●●●●●●●●●●●●●●●●●●●●●●●●●●●●●●●●●●●●

National Association of Social Workers, Standards for the Private Practice of Clinical Social Work

Qualifications for the Clinical Social Worker in Private Practice

I. The clinical social worker in private practice shall meet the educational and practice requirements of the National Association of Social Workers, shall maintain current knowledge of scientific and professional developments, and shall obtain additional training when required for effective practice.

A. The practitioner shall have a Master's or Doctoral degree from an accredited school of social work plus two years or 3,000 hours of post-degree direct practice experience, supervised by a Master's level clinical social worker, in a hospital, clinic, agency, or other institutional setting.

B. The practitioner shall abide by NASW's continuing education requirements and other standards relating to competence in clinical practice which shall be established by the Association.

C. The clinical social worker practicing privately for the first time should obtain consultation from an experienced clinical social worker.

D. The practitioner shall limit the practice to demonstrated areas of professional competence.

E. When using specialized methods of practice which range

National Association of Social Workers, *Standards for the Private Practice of Clinical Social Work* (Washington, D.C.: National Association of Social Workers, draft of April 22, 1981).

beyond those normally learned in a school of social work or social work practice setting, the practitioner shall obtain training or professional supervision in the modalities employed.

Legal Aspects of Private Clinical Practice

II. The clinical social worker in private practice shall comply with the laws of the jurisdiction within which s/he practices. The practitioner shall adhere to the educational, experiential, and other practice requirements of law in those jurisdictions which regulate clinical social work.

Professional Identification and Commitment

III. The privately practicing clinician whose training is in social work: (a) identifies himself/herself as a member of the social work profession, regardless of clinical orientation; and (b) is committed to the profession.
  A. Commitment to the profession is demonstrated through organizational participation, teaching, writing, and other activities.
  B. The practitioner should belong to the NASW, ACSW, the NASW Register of Clinical Social Workers and shall adhere to the NASW Code of Ethics.
  C. The privately practicing clinical social worker, like all social workers, should seek modification within the client and within those societal systems and institutions which affect the client.
  D. The practitioner shall be subject to NASW standards and grievance procedures and to peer and utilization review depending upon state and local law and customary professional practice.

The Maintenance of Confidentiality

IV. The clinical social worker in private practice shall abide by the provisions of confidentiality in the NASW Code of Ethics. (See Appendix I.)

A. The social worker should share with others confidences revealed by clients, without their consent, only for compelling professional reasons.

Duty to
Warn

1. The clinical social worker in private practice may find it necessary to reveal confidential information disclosed by the patient to protect the patient or the community from imminent danger.
2. When the clinical social worker in private practice is ordered by the court to reveal the confidences entrusted by patients, the practitioner may comply or may ethically hold the right to dissent within the framework of the law.

The Management Aspects of a Private Clinical Practice

V. To render the best possible service to the client, the clinical social worker shall be capable of managing the business aspects of a private practice.

A. The clinical practitioner shall be familiar with relevant state and local laws on the conduct of a business.
B. The practitioner should carry malpractice and premises liability insurance.
C. The practitioner shall deal expediently and efficiently with insurance companies covering clinical social work services. This includes maintenance of records and the use of diagnostic categories in billing private and governmental carriers.

Contracts

D. The private practitioner and client shall agree to a contract during the initial visit(s). Conditions of the contract shall be clear and explicit. These shall include:

1. Agreement about fees; insurance; length, frequency, and location of sessions; appointments missed or cancelled without adequate notice; vacation coverage during an absence; collateral contacts. (The foregoing information may be provided on a standardized form.)
2. Agreement regarding goals of treatment.
3. Informing the client of his/her rights.

Records

E. Private clinical practitioners shall keep up-to-date, accurate records on the treatment of the client. (Records should protect confidentiality while recording subjects discussed in sufficient detail to justify therapeutic action.)

F. Offices in which services are rendered shall be located for client safety, accessibility, and privacy.

G. A social worker in private practice may advertise. The advertisement should clearly inform a prospective client of the nature of the services to be received. Advertisements shall not misrepresent qualifications, competence, service, or results to be achieved. (See Code of Ethics V.M.4.)

H. When a clinical social worker terminates a private practice, there is a responsibility to refer clients elsewhere. If the clinical social worker chooses, s/he may carefully select a successor to whom the practice may be sold. Clients should be given the choice of transferring to the successor or to another clinician. The responsible practitioner collaborates with the successor for the maximum benefit of their mutual clients. *Termination*

I. The privately practicing clinical social worker's rates shall be commensurate with services performed and with fees charged by mental health professionals practicing in the community. Clients who cannot pay the practitioner's fee should be referred to a mental health or family agency or to a private practitioner with lower rates.

J. The practitioner's bill shall reflect services actually rendered.

K. The clinical social worker shall not divide a fee or accept or give anything of value for receiving or making a referral. (See Code of Ethics II.I.1.)

L. Unpaid accounts may be collected through a collection agency [or] small claims court or through other legal action when efforts to collect directly from the client have failed.

Modalities and Methods of Treatment

VI. A variety of professionally acceptable and ethically sanctioned modalities and methods of treatment may be used in the private practice of clinical social work.

Drugs
A. The practitioner shall be familiar with the client's physical condition, collaborating with a physician when the client is chronically ill or disabled and/or using medication. The practitioner shall refer the client to a physician for treatment or medication when necessary.
B. The privately practicing clinical social worker may certify or admit clients to institutional facilities depending upon state law or local practice.
C. An appointment with a relative or collateral shall be made only when the client's permission has been obtained.
D. The privately practicing clinical social worker shall not discriminate against or refuse to treat a client because of race, sex, color, sexual orientation, religion, lifestyle, mental or physical handicap. (See Code of Ethics II.F.3.)
E. The private practice may be limited to certain specialties but clients outside the practitioner's area of expertise should be referred to appropriate resources.

Sex as
Therapy
F. The private practitioner shall not engage in sexual activities with clients. (See Code of Ethics II.F.5.)

Duty to
Consult
G. Clients should be treated as expeditiously as possible. Consultation should be sought when there is a lack of progress in treatment.

*Relationships with Other Professionals
and Community Agencies*

VII. The privately practicing clinical social worker shall maintain the highest professional and business ethics in dealing with other professionals and community agencies.
A. The practitioner shall be familiar with the network of professional and self-help systems in the community and shall link clients with relevant services and resources.
B. When the client is referred to another resource, the role of the primary provider of care and the specific responsibility of each party concerned with the client should be delineated clearly.
C. When the clinical social worker is unable to continue

service to an individual(s), there is a responsibility to offer suitable referral(s).

D. The practitioner shall cooperate with professionals who subsequently treat former clients.
E. The clinical social worker leaving an agency for private practice shall abide by that agency's explicit policy regarding transfer of clients. If the agency permits transfer of the client to a private practice, there shall be advance agreement between the agency and the practitioner before discussing options with the client.
F. The clinical social worker employing others in the private practice shall assume professional responsibility and accountability for all services provided.

APPENDIX I

Confidentiality and Privacy—The social worker should respect the privacy of clients and hold in confidence all information obtained in the course of professional service.

The social worker should share with others confidences revealed by clients, without consent, only for compelling professional reasons.

The social worker should inform clients fully about the limits of confidentiality in a given situation, the purposes for which information is obtained, and how it may be used.

The social worker should afford clients reasonable access to any official social work records concerning them.

When providing clients with access to records, the social worker should take due care to protect the confidences of others contained in those records.

The social worker should obtain informed consent of clients before taping, recording, or permitting third party observation of their activities.

C

●●●●●●●●●●●●●●●●●●●●●●●●●●●●●●●●●●●●●●

*American Association for Marriage
and Family Therapy,
Code of Professional Ethics*

Section I. Code of Personal Conduct

1. A therapist provides professional service to anyone regardless of race, religion, sex, political affiliation, social or economic status, or choice of lifestyle. When a therapist cannot offer service for any reason, he or she will make proper referral. Therapists are encouraged to devote a portion of their time to work for which there is little or no financial return.

Fiduciary
Duty

2. A therapist will not use his or her counseling relationship to further personal, religious, political, or business interests.

3. A therapist will neither offer nor accept payment for referrals, and will actively seek all significant information from the source of referral.

4. A therapist will not knowingly offer service to a client who is in treatment with another clinical professional without consultation among the parties involved.

5. A therapist will not disparage the qualifications of any colleague.

6. Every member of the AAMFT has an obligation to continuing education and professional growth in all possible ways, including active participation in the meetings and affairs of the Association.

7. A therapist will not attempt to diagnose, prescribe for,

American Association for Marriage and Family Therapy (AAMFT), *Code of Professional Ethics* (Claremont, Calif.: AAMFT, n.d.).

treat, or advise on problems outside the recognized boundaries of the therapist's competence.

8. A therapist will attempt to avoid relationships with clients which might impair professional judgment or increase the risks of exploiting clients. Examples of such relationships include: treatment of family members, close friends, employees, or supervisees. Sexual intimacy with clients is unethical.   *Undue Influence*

   Sex as Innovative Therapy

9. The AAMFT encourages its members to affiliate with professional groups, clinics, or agencies operating in the field of marriage and family life. Similarly, interdisciplinary contact and cooperation are encouraged.

Section II. Relations with Clients

1. A therapist, while offering dignified and reasonable support, is cautious in prognosis and will not exaggerate the efficacy of his or her services.   *Warranty*

2. The therapist recognizes the importance of clear understandings on financial matters with clients. Arrangements for payments are settled at the beginning of a therapeutic relationship.   *Contract*

3. A therapist keeps records of each case and stores them in such a way as to insure safety and confidentiality, in accordance with the highest professional and legal standards.

   a. Information shall be revealed only to professional persons concerned with the case. Written and oral reports should present only data germane to the purposes of the inquiry; every effort should be made to avoid undue invasion of privacy.

   b. The therapist is responsible for informing clients of the limits of confidentiality.   *Informed Consent*

   c. Written permission shall be granted by the clients involved before data may be divulged.

   d. Information is not communicated to others without consent of the client unless there is clear and immediate danger to an individual or to society, and then only to the appropriate family members, professional workers, or public authorities.   *Duty to Warn*

4. A therapist deals with relationships at varying stages of their history. While respecting at all times the rights of clients to make their own decisions, the therapist has a duty to assess the situation according to the highest professional standards. In all circumstances, the therapist will clearly advise a client that the decision to separate or divorce is the responsibility solely of the client. In such an event, the therapist has the continuing responsibility to offer support and counsel during the period of readjustment.

Undue
Influence

Section III. Research and Publication
1. The therapist is obligated to protect the welfare of his or her research subjects. The conditions of the Human Subjects Experimentation shall prevail, as specified by the Department of Health, Education and Welfare guidelines.
2. Publication credit is assigned to those who have contributed to a publication, in proportion to their contribution, and in accordance with customary publication practices.

Section IV. Implementation
1. In accepting membership in the Association, each member binds himself or herself to accept the judgment of fellow members as to standards of professional ethics, subject to the safeguards provided in this section. Acceptance of membership implies consent to abide by the acts of discipline herein set forth and as enumerated in the Bylaws of the Association. It is the duty of each member to safeguard these standards of ethical practice. Should a fellow member appear to violate this Code, he or she may be cautioned through friendly remonstrance, colleague consultation with the party in question, or formal complaint may be filed in accordance with the following procedure:
   a. Complaint of unethical practice shall be made in writing to the Chairperson of the Standing Committee on Ethics and Professional Practices and to the Executive Director. A copy of the complaint shall be furnished to the person or persons against whom it is directed.
   b. Should the Standing Committee decide the complaint warrants investigation, it shall so notify the charged

party(ies) in writing. When investigation is indicated, the Standing Committee shall constitute itself an Investigating Committee and shall include in its membership at least one member of the Board and at least two members (other than the charging or charged parties or any possible witnesses) from the local area involved. This Investigating Committee or representatives thereof shall make one or more local visits of investigation of the complaint. After full investigation following due process and offering the charged party(ies) opportunity to defend him or herself, the Committee shall report its findings and recommendations to the Board of Directors for action.

c. The charged party(ies) shall have free access to all charges and evidence cited against him or her, and shall have full freedom to defend himself or herself before the Investigating Committee and the Board, including the right to legal counsel.

d. Recommendation made by the Committee shall be:
   1. Advice that the charges be dropped as unfounded.
   2. Specified admonishment.
   3. Reprimand.
   4. Dismissal from membership.

2. Should a member of this Association be expelled, he or she shall at once surrender his or her membership certificate to the Board of Directors. Failure to do so shall result in such action as legal counsel may recommend.

3. Should a member of this Association be expelled from another recognized professional association or his/her state license revoked for unethical conduct, the Standing Committee on Ethics shall investigate the matter and, where appropriate, act in the manner provided above respecting charges of unethical conduct.

4. The Committee will also give due consideration to a formal complaint by a non-member.

Section V. Public Information and Advertising
   All professional presentations to the public will be governed by the Standards on Public Information and Advertising.

STANDARDS ON PUBLIC INFORMATION
AND ADVERTISING

Section I. General Principles

The practice of marriage and family therapy as a mental health profession is in the public interest. Therefore, it is appropriate for the well-trained and qualified practitioner to inform the public of the availability of his/her services. However, much needs to be done to educate the public as to the services available from qualified marriage and family therapists. Therefore, the clinical members of AAMFT have a responsibility to the public to engage in appropriate informational activities and to avoid misrepresentation or misleading statements in keeping with the following general principles and specific regulations.

Selection of a Marriage and Family Therapist

    A. At a time when the Human Services field is burgeoning and becoming increasingly complex and specialized, few marriage and family therapists are willing and competent to deal with every kind of marital or family problem, and many laypersons have difficulty in determining the competence of psychotherapists in general and marriage and family therapists in particular to render different types of services. The selection of a marriage and family therapist is particularly difficult for transients, persons moving into new areas, persons of limited education or means, and others who have had no previous experience or the degree of sophistication required to evaluate training and competence or because they are in some sort of crisis.

    B. Selection of a marriage and family therapist by a layperson should be made on an informed basis. Advice and recommendation of third parties—physicians, other professionals, relatives, friends, acquaintances, business associates—and restrained publicity may be helpful. A marriage and family therapist should not compensate another person for recommending him/her, for influencing a prospective client to employ him/her, or to encourage future recommendations. Advertisements and public communications, whether in directories, announcement cards, newspapers, or on radio or television, should be formulated to convey information that is necessary to make an appropriate selection. Self-praising should be avoided. Information that may be helpful in some situations would include: (1) office information, such as name, including a group name and names of professional associates, address, telephone number, credit card acceptability, languages spoken and written, and office hours; (2) earned degrees, state licensure and/or certification, and AAMFT clinical membership status; (3) description of practice, including a statement that practice is limited to one or more fields of marriage and family therapy; and (4) permitted fee information.

C. The proper motivation for commercial publicity by marriage and family therapists lies in the need to inform the public of the availability of competent, independent marriage and family therapists. The public benefit derived from advertising depends upon the usefulness of the information provided to the community to which it is directed. Advertising marked by excesses of content, volume, scope, or frequency, or which unduly emphasizes unrepresentative biographical information, does not provide that public benefit. The use of media whose scope or nature clearly suggests that the use is intended for self-praising of the therapist without concomitant benefit to the public distorts the legitimate purpose of informing the public and is clearly improper. Indeed, this and other improper advertising may hinder informed selection of a competent, independent professional and advertising that involves excessive cost may unnecessarily increase fees for marriage and family therapy.

D. Advertisements and other communications should make it apparent that the necessity [for] and advisability of marriage and family therapy depend on variant factors that must be evaluated individually. Because fee information frequently may be incomplete and misleading to a layperson, a marriage and family therapist should exer-

cise great care to assure that fee information is complete and accurate. Because of the individuality of each
problem, public statements regarding average, minimum,
or estimated fees may be deceiving as will commercial
publicity conveying information as to results previously
achieved, general or average solutions, or expected outcomes. It would be misleading to advertise a set fee for
a specific type of case without adhering to the stated
fee in charging clients. Advertisements or public claims
that use statistical data or other information based on
past performance or prediction of future success may
be deceptive if they ignore important variables. Only
factual assertions, and not opinions, should be made in
public communications. Not only must commercial
publicity be truthful but its accurate meaning must be
Warranty   apparent to the average layperson. No guarantees about
the outcomes of therapy should be made or implied.
Any commercial publicity or advertising for which payment is made should so indicate unless it is apparent
from the context that it is paid publicity or an advertisement.

E. The desirability of affording the public access to information relevant to their needs and problems has resulted
in some relaxation of the former restrictions against advertising by marriage and family therapists. Historically,
those restrictions were imposed to prevent deceptive
publicity that would mislead laypersons, cause distrust
of the profession, and undermine public confidence in
the profession, and all marriage and family therapists
should remain vigilant to prevent such results. Ambiguous information relevant to a layperson's decision regarding his/her selection of a marriage and family therapist, provided in ways that do not comport with the
dignity of the profession or which demean the amelior-
ation of human problems, is inappropriate in public
communications. The regulation of advertising by marriage and family therapists is rooted in the public interest. Advertising through which a marriage and family

therapist seeks business by use of extravagant or brash statements or appeals to fears could mislead and harm the layperson. Furthermore, public communications that would produce unrealistic expectations in particular cases and bring about distrust of the profession would be harmful to society. Thus, public confidence in our profession would be impaired by such advertisements of professional services. The therapist-client relationship, being personal and unique, should not be established as the result of pressures, deceptions, or exploitation of the vulnerability of clients frequently experiencing significant stress at the time they seek help.

F. The Regulations recognize the value of giving assistance in the selection process through forms of advertising that furnish identification of a marriage and family therapist while avoiding falsity, deception, and misrep-   Fraud
resentation. All publicity should be evaluated with regard to its effects on the layperson. The layperson is best served if advertisements contain no misleading information or emotional appeals, and emphasize the necessity of an individualized evaluation of the situation before conclusions as to need for a particular type of therapy and probable expenses can be made. The therapist-client relationship should result from a free and informed choice by the layperson. Unwarranted promises of benefits, over-persuasion, or vexatious or harassing conduct is improper.

G. The name under which a marriage and family therapist conducts his/her practice may be a factor in the selection process. The use of a name which could mislead laypersons concerning the identity, responsibility, source, and status of those practicing thereunder is not proper. Likewise, one should not hold oneself out as being a partner or associate of a firm if he/she is not one in fact.

H. In order to avoid the possibility of misleading persons with whom he/she deals, a marriage and family therapist should be scrupulous in the representation of his/her professional background, training, and status. In some instances a marriage and family therapist confines his/her practice to a particular area within the field of marriage and family therapy. However, a member should not hold himself/herself out as a specialist without evidence of training, education, and supervised experience in settings which meet recognized professional standards. A marriage and family therapist may, however, indicate, if it is factual, a limitation of his/her practice or that he/she practices within one or more particular areas of marriage and family treatment in public pronouncements which will assist laypersons in selecting a marriage and family therapist and accurately describe the limited area in which the member practices.

Standard
of a
Specialty

I. The marriage and family therapist should support the creation and evolution of ethical, approved plans (such as marriage and family therapist referral systems) which aid in the selection of qualified therapists.

Section II. Regulations

A. The American Association for Marriage and Family Therapy is the sole owner of its name, its logo, and the abbreviated initials AAMFT. Use of the name, logo, and initials is restricted to the following conditions.

1. Only individual clinical members may identify their membership in AAMFT in public information or advertising materials, not associates or students of organizations.

2. The initials AAMFT may not be used following one's name in the manner of an academic degree because this is misleading.

3. Use of the logo is limited to the association, its committees and regional divisions when they are engaged in bona fide activities as units or divisions of AAMFT.

4. A regional division or chapter of AAMFT may use the AAMFT insignia to list its individual members as a group (e.g., in the Yellow Pages). When all Clinical Members practicing within a directory district have

been invited to list, any one or more member may do so.

B. A marriage and family therapist shall not knowingly make a representation about his/her ability, background, or experience, or that of a partner or associate, or about the fee or any other aspect of a proposed professional engagement, that is false, fraudulent, mislead-leading, or deceptive, and that might reasonably be expected to induce reliance by a member of the public.

C. Without limitation, a false, fraudulent, misleading, or deceptive statement or claim includes a statement or claim which:

    Fraud

1. Contains a material misrepresentation of fact;
2. Omits to state any material fact necessary to make the statement, in light of all circumstances, not misleading;
3. Is intended or is likely to create an unjustified expectation;
4. Relates to professional fees other than:
    (a) a statement of the fee for an initial consultation;
    (b) a statement of the fee charges for a specific service, the description of which would not be misunderstood or be deceptive;
    (c) a statement of the range of fees for specifically described services, provided there is a reasonable disclosure of all relevant variables and considerations so that the statement would not be misunderstood or be deceptive;
    (d) a statement of specified hourly rates, provided the statement makes clear that the total charge will vary according to the number of hours devoted to the matter;
    (e) the availability of credit arrangements; or
5. Contains a representation or implication that is likely to cause an ordinary prudent person to misunderstand or be deceived or fails to contain reasonable warnings or disclaimers necessary to make a representation or implication not deceptive.

D. A member shall not, on his/her own behalf or on behalf of a partner or associate or any other therapist associated with the firm, use or participate in the use of any form of advertising of services which:
1. Contains statistical data or other information based on past performance or prediction of future success;
2. Contains a testimonial about or endorsement of a therapist;
3. Contains a statement of opinion as to the quality of the services or contains a representation or implication regarding the quality of services, whether therapeutic or educational, which is not susceptible of reasonable verification by the public;
4. Is intended or is likely to attract clients by use of showmanship or self-praising.

E. A member shall not compensate or give anything of value to a representative of the press, radio, television, or other communication medium in anticipation of or in return for professional publicity in a news item. A paid advertisement must be identified as such unless it is apparent from the context that it is a paid advertisement. If the paid advertisement is communicated to the public by use of radio or television, it shall be prerecorded, approved for broadcast by the therapist, and a recording of the actual transmission shall be retained by the therapist.

PROFESSIONAL NOTICES, LETTERHEADS, OFFICES, AND DIRECTORY LISTINGS

F. A member or group of members shall not use or participate in the use of a professional card, professional announcement card, office sign, letterhead, telephone directory listing, association directory listing, or a similar professional notice or device if it includes a statement or claim that is false, fraudulent, misleading, or deceptive within the meaning of Section II, C or that violates the regulations contained in Section II, D.

Fraud   G. A member shall not practice under a name that is misleading as to the identity, responsibility, or status of those practicing thereunder, or is otherwise false, fraudulent, misleading, or deceptive within the meaning of Section II, C or is contrary to law. However, the name of a professional corporation or professional association may contain "P.C." or "P.A." or similar symbols indicating the nature of the organization.

H. A member shall not hold himself/herself out as having a partnership with one or more other qualified therapists unless they are in fact partners.

I. A partnership shall not be formed or continued between or among members in different geographical locations unless all enumerations of the members or associates of the firm on its letterhead and in other permissible listings make clear the limitations due to geographical separation of the members or associates of the firm.

J. Academic degrees earned from institutions accredited by regionally or nationally recognized accrediting agencies or associations may be used or permitted to be used provided that the statement or claim is neither false, fraudulent, misleading, or deceptive within the meaning of Section II, C.

SOLICITATION OF PROFESSIONAL EMPLOYMENT

K. A member shall not seek, by in-person contact, his/her employment as a therapist (or employment of a partner or associate) by a client who has not sought his/her advice regarding employment of a marriage and family therapist if:

1. The solicitation involves use of a statement or claim that is false, fraudulent, misleading, or deceptive within the meaning of Section II, C; or

2. The solicitation involves the use of undue influence; or

    Undue Influence

3. The potential client is apparently in a physical or mental condition which would make it unlikely that he or she could exercise reasonable, considered judg-

ment as to the selection of a marriage and family therapist.

L. A member shall not compensate or give anything of value to a person or organization to recommend or secure his/her employment by a claim or as a reward for having made a recommendation resulting in his/her employment by a client.

M. A member shall not accept employment when he/she knows or it is obvious that the person who seeks his/her service does so as a result of conduct prohibited by this Section.

SUGGESTION OF NEED OF MARRIAGE OR FAMILY THERAPY

N. A member who has given unsolicited advice to a layperson that he/she/they should obtain marriage or family therapy shall not accept employment resulting from that advice if:

Fraud

1. The advice embodies or implies a statement or claim that is false, fraudulent, misleading, or deceptive within the meaning of Section II, C or that violates the regulations contained in Section II, D; or

Warranty

2. The advice involves the use by the marriage and family therapist of coercion, duress, compulsion, intimidation, unwarranted promises of benefits, overreaching, [or] vexatious or harassing conduct.

D

●●●●●●●●●●●●●●●●●●●●●●●●●●●●●●●●

American Psychiatric Association, Principles of Medical Ethics, with Annotations Especially Applicable to Psychiatry

Section 1

A physician shall be dedicated to providing competent medical service with compassion and respect for human dignity.

1. The patient may place his/her trust in his/her psychiatrist knowing that the psychiatrist's ethics and professional responsibilities preclude him/her gratifying his/her own needs by exploiting the patient. This becomes particularly important because of the essentially private, highly personal, and sometimes intensely emotional nature of the relationship established with the psychiatrist.

   Fiduciary Duty

2. A psychiatrist should not be a party to any type of policy that excludes, segregates, or demeans the dignity of any patient because of ethnic origin, race, sex, creed, age, socioeconomic status, or sexual orientation.

3. In accord with the requirements of law and accepted medical practice, it is ethical for a physician to submit his/her work to peer review and to the ultimate authority of the medical staff executive body and the hospital administration and its governing body. In case of dispute, the ethical psychiatrist has the following steps available:

Reprinted from *Principles of Medical Ethics, with Annotations Especially Applicable to Psychiatry* (Washington, D.C.: American Psychiatric Association, 1981). Statements in italics are taken directly from the American Medical Association's Principles of Medical Ethics.

    a. Seek appeal from the medical staff decision to a joint conference committee, including members of the medical staff executive committee and the executive committee of the governing board. At this appeal, the ethical psychiatrist could request that outside opinions be considered.

    b. Appeal to the governing body itself.

    c. Appeal to state agencies regulating licensure of hospitals if, in the particular state, they concern themselves with matters of professional competency and quality of care.

    d. Attempt to educate colleagues through development of research projects and data and presentations at professional meetings and in professional journals.

    e. Seek redress in local courts, perhaps through an enjoining injunction against the governing body.

    f. Public education as carried out by an ethical psychiatrist would not utilize appeals based solely upon emotion, but would be presented in a professional way and without any potential exploitation of patients through testimonials.

4. A psychiatrist should not be a participant in a legally authorized execution.

Section 2

A physician shall deal honestly with patients and colleagues, and strive to expose those physicians deficient in character or competence, or who engage in fraud or deception.

1. The requirement that the physician conduct himself with propriety in his/her profession and in all the actions of his/her life is especially important in the case of the psychiatrist because the patient tends to model his/her behavior after that of his/her therapist by identification. Further, the necessary intensity of the therapeutic relationship may tend to activate sexual and other needs and fantasies on the part of both patient and therapist, while weakening the objectivity necessary for control. Sexual activity with a patient is unethical.

Sex as Innovative Therapy

2. The psychiatrist should diligently guard against exploiting information furnished by the patient and should not use the unique position of power afforded him/her by the psycho-

Undue Influence

therapeutic situation to influence the patient in any way not directly relevant to the treatment goals.

3. A psychiatrist who regularly practices outside his/her area of professional competence should be considered unethical. Determination of professional competence should be made by peer review boards or other appropriate bodies.

4. Special consideration should be given to those psychiatrists who, because of mental illness, jeopardize the welfare of their patients and their own reputations and practices. It is ethical, even encouraged, for another psychiatrist to intercede in such situations.

5. Psychiatric services, like all medical services, are dispensed in the context of a contractual arrangement between the patient and the treating physician. The provisions of the contractual arrangement, which are binding on the physician as well as on the patient, should be explicitly established.   Contract

6. It is ethical for the psychiatrist to make a charge for a missed appointment when this falls within the terms of the specific contractual agreement with the patient. Charging for a missed appointment or for one not cancelled 24 hours in advance need not, in itself, be considered unethical if a patient is fully advised that the physician will make such a charge. The practice, however, should be resorted to infrequently and always with the utmost consideration of the patient and his/her circumstances.

7. An arrangement in which a psychiatrist provides supervision or administration to other physicians or nonmedical persons for a percentage of their fees or gross income is not acceptable; this would constitute fee-splitting. In a team of practitioners, or a multidisciplinary team, it is ethical for the psychiatrist to receive income for administration, research, education, or consultation. This should be based upon a mutually agreed upon and set fee or salary, open to renegotiation when a change in the time demand occurs. (See also Section 5, Annotations 2, 3, and 4.)

8. When a member has been found to have behaved unethically by the American Psychiatric Association or one of its constituent district branches, there should not be automatic re-

porting to the local authorities responsible for medical licensure, but the decision to report should be decided upon the merits of the case.

Section 3

A physician shall respect the law and also recognize a responsibility to seek changes in those requirements which are contrary to the best interests of the patient.

1. It would seem self-evident that a psychiatrist who is a lawbreaker might be ethically unsuited to practice his/her profession. When such illegal activities bear directly upon his/her practice, this would obviously be the case. However, in other instances, illegal activities such as those concerning the right to protest social injustices might not bear on either the image of the psychiatrist or the ability of the specific psychiatrist to treat his/her patient ethically and well. While no committee or board could offer prior assurance that any illegal activity would not be considered unethical, it is conceivable that an individual could violate a law without being guilty of professionally unethical behavior. Physicians lose no right of citizenship on entry into the profession of medicine.
2. Where not specifically prohibited by local laws governing medical practice, the practice of acupuncture by a psychiatrist is not unethical per se. The psychiatrist should have professional competence in the use of acupuncture. Or, if he/she is supervising the use of acupuncture by nonmedical individuals, he/she should provide proper medical supervision. (See also Section 5, Annotations 3 and 4.)

Section 4

A physician shall respect the rights of patients, of colleagues, and of other health professionals, and shall safeguard patient confidences within the constraints of the law.

1. Psychiatric records, including even the identification of a person as a patient, must be protected with extreme care. Confidentiality is essential to psychiatric treatment. This is based

in part on the special nature of psychiatric therapy as well as on the traditional ethical relationship between physician and patient. Growing concern regarding the civil rights of patients and the possible adverse effects of computerization, duplication equipment, and data banks makes the dissemination of confidential information an increasing hazard. Because of the sensitive and private nature of the information with which the psychiatrist deals, he/she must be circumspect in the information that he/she chooses to disclose to others about a patient. The welfare of the patient must be a continuing consideration.

2. A psychiatrist may release confidential information only with the authorization of the patient or under proper legal compulsion. The continuing duty of the psychiatrist to protect the patient includes fully apprising him/her of the connotations of waiving the privilege of privacy. This may become an issue when the patient is being investigated by a government agency, is applying for a position, or is involved in legal action. The same principles apply to the release of information concerning treatment to medical departments of government agencies, business organizations, labor unions, and insurance companies. Information gained in confidence about patients seen in student health services should not be released without the student's explicit permission. *Informed Consent*

3. Clinical and other materials used in teaching and writing must be adequately disguised in order to preserve the anonymity of the individuals involved.

4. The ethical responsibility of maintaining confidentiality holds equally for the consultations in which the patient may not have been present and in which the consultee was not a physician. In such instances, the physician consultant should alert the consultee to his/her duty of confidentiality.

5. Ethically the psychiatrist may disclose only that information which is relevant to a given situation. He/she should avoid offering speculation as fact. Sensitive information such as an individual's sexual orientation or fantasy material is usually unnecessary. *Records*

6. Psychiatrists are often asked to examine individuals for secur-

Informed
Consent

ity purposes, to determine suitability for various jobs, and to determine legal competence. The psychiatrist must fully describe the nature and purpose and lack of confidentiality of the examination to the examinee at the beginning of the examination.

7. Careful judgment must be exercised by the psychiatrist in order to include, when appropriate, the parents or guardian in the treatment of a minor. At the same time the psychiatrist must assure the minor proper confidentiality.

Duty to
Warn

8. Psychiatrists at times may find it necessary, in order to protect the patient or the community from imminent danger, to reveal confidential information disclosed by the patient.

9. When the psychiatrist is ordered by the court to reveal the confidences entrusted to him/her by patients, he/she may comply or he/she may ethically hold the right to dissent within the framework of the law. When the psychiatrist is in doubt, the right of the patient to confidentiality and, by extension, to unimpaired treatment should be given priority. The psychiatrist should reserve the right to raise the question of adequate need for disclosure. In the event that the necessity for legal disclosure is demonstrated by the court, the psychiatrist may request the right to disclosure of only that information which is relevant to the legal question at hand.

Informed
Consent

10. With regard for the person's dignity and privacy and with truly informed consent, it is ethical to present a patient to a scientific gathering, if the confidentiality of the presentation is understood and accepted by the audience.

Informed
Consent

11. It is ethical to present a patient or former patient to a public gathering or to the news media only if that patient is fully informed of enduring loss of confidentiality, is competent, and consents in writing without coercion.

12. When involved in funded research, the ethical psychiatrist will advise human subjects of the funding source, retain his/her freedom to reveal data and results, and follow all appropriate and current guidelines relative to human subject protection.

13. Ethical considerations in medical practice preclude the psy-

chiatric evaluation of any adult charged with criminal acts prior to access to, or availability of, legal counsel. The only exception is the rendering of care to the person for the sole purpose of medical treatment.

Section 5

A physician shall continue to study, apply, and advance scientific knowledge, make relevant information available to patients, colleagues, and the public, obtain consultation, and use the talents of other health professionals when indicated.

1. Psychiatrists are responsible for their own continuing education and should be mindful of the fact that theirs must be a lifetime of learning.
2. In the practice of his/her specialty, the psychiatrist consults, associates, collaborates, or integrates his/her work with that of many professionals, including psychologists, psychometricians, social workers, alcoholism counselors, marriage counselors, public health nurses, etc. Furthermore, the nature of modern psychiatric practice extends his/her contacts to such people as teachers, juvenile and adult probation officers, attorneys, welfare workers, agency volunteers, and neighborhood aids. In referring patients for treatment, counseling, or rehabilitation to any of these practitioners, the psychiatrist should ensure that the allied professional or paraprofessional with whom he/she is dealing is a recognized member of his/her own discipline and is competent to carry out the therapeutic task required. The psychiatrist should have the same attitude toward members of the medical profession to whom he/she refers patients. Whenever he/she has reason to doubt the training, skill, or ethical qualifications of the allied professional, the psychiatrist should not refer cases to him/her.
3. When the psychiatrist assumes a collaborative or supervisory role with another mental health worker, he/she must expend sufficient time to assure that proper care is given. It is contrary to the interests of the patient and to patient care if he/she allows himself/herself to be used as a figurehead. *Supervision*
4. In relationships between psychiatrists and practicing licensed

psychologists, the physician should not delegate to the psychologist or, in fact, to any nonmedical person any matter requiring the exercise of professional medical judgment.

Consultation

5. The psychiatrist should agree to the request of a patient for consultation or to such a request from the family of an incompetent or minor patient. The psychiatrist may suggest possible consultants, but the patient or family should be given free choice of the consultant. If the psychiatrist disapproves of the professional qualifications of the consultant or if there is a difference of opinion that the primary therapist cannot resolve, he/she may, after suitable notice, withdraw from the case. If this disagreement occurs within an institution or agency framework, the difference should be resolved by the mediation or arbitration of higher professional authority within the institution or agency.

Section 6

A physician shall, in the provision of appropriate patient care, except in emergencies, be free to choose whom to serve, with whom to associate, and the environment in which to provide medical services.

Termination

1. Physicians generally agree that the doctor-patient relationship is such a vital factor in effective treatment of the patient that preservation of optimal conditions for development of a sound working relationship between a doctor and his/her patient should take precedence over all other considerations. Professional courtesy may lead to poor psychiatric care for physicians and their families because of embarrassment over the lack of a complete give-and-take contract.

Section 7

A physician shall recognize a responsibility to participate in activities contributing to an improved community.

1. Psychiatrists should foster the cooperation of those legitimately concerned with the medical, psychological, social, and legal aspects of mental health and illness. Psychiatrists are en-

couraged to serve society by advising and consulting with the executive, legislative, and judiciary branches of the government. A psychiatrist should clarify whether he/she speaks as an individual or as a representative of an organization. Furthermore, psychiatrists should avoid cloaking their public statements with the authority of the profession (e.g., "Psychiatrists know that . . .").

2. Psychiatrists may interpret and share with the public their expertise in the various psychosocial issues that may affect mental health and illness. Psychiatrists should always be mindful of their separate roles as dedicated citizens and as experts in psychological medicine.

3. On occasion psychiatrists are asked for an opinion about an individual who is in the light of public attention, or who has disclosed information about himself/herself through public media. It is unethical for a psychiatrist to offer a professional opinion unless he/she has conducted an examination and has been granted proper authorization for such a statement.

4. The psychiatrist may permit his/her certification to be used for the involuntary treatment of any person only following his/her personal examination of that person. To do so, he/she must find that the person, because of mental illness, cannot form a judgment as to what is in his/her own best interests and that, without such treatment, substantial impairment is likely to occur to the person or others.

Commitment

E

●●●●●●●●●●●●●●●●●●●●●●●●●●●●●●●●●●●●●●

American Psychiatric Association (Task Force on Electroconvulsive Therapy), Recommendations Regarding the Use of Electroconvulsive Therapy

In formulating the following we emphasize that

(i) Clinical diagnosis of psychiatric disorders is not yet precise and absolute but is developing.

(ii) There is insufficient evidence to support exclusively any one preferred sequence of treatments in psychiatry.

(iii) The techniques of ECT are evolving and differ today from what they were during the first two decades after its introduction, e.g., the routine use now of anesthesia, oxygenation, and muscle relaxation. Further, the placement of both electrodes over the right hemisphere in right-handed patients (non-dominant unilateral ECT) has been demonstrated as an effective treatment with considerably less memory impairment compared with bilateral electrode placement.

(iv) Indications for the use of ECT have been more sharply defined.

(v) The dangers of alternative therapies can be considerable.

I. Indications
  A. ECT is an effective treatment in cases of:
    (1) severe depression where the risk of suicide is high and/or where the patient is not taking adequate

Reprinted from *Report of the Task Force on Electroconvulsive Therapy* (Washington, D.C. American Psychiatric Association, 1978).

food or fluids and/or where the use of drug or other therapy entails high risks and/or will take an unacceptably long period to manifest a therapeutic response;

(2) severe psychoses characterized by behavior which is a threat to the safety and well-being of the patient and/or others and which cannot be controlled by drugs or other means, or for which drugs cannot be employed because of adverse reactions or because of the risks which their use entails;

(3) severe catatonia which has not responded to drugs and/or where the patient is not taking food or fluids and/or where drug therapy or other means entail unacceptable risks;

(4) severe mania where the use of drug therapy entails unacceptable risks and/or where coexisting medical problems (e.g., recent myocardial infarction) either require prompt resolution of the mania and/or make the use of drug therapy unacceptable.

B. ECT is probably effective in:

(1) depressions, particularly those characterized by vegetative or endogenous symptoms, which have not responded satisfactorily to an adequate course of therapy with antidepressant drugs;

(2) depressions, particularly those with vegetative or endogenous elements, in which the use of drug therapy is contraindicated;

(3) psychoses, and particularly those with an endogenous affective component, which have not responded to an adequate trial of anti-psychotic drugs or where drugs cannot be used because of adverse reactions.

C. There exists among some psychiatrists the opinion that ECT is an appropriate treatment for conditions other than the affective disorders and schizophrenia. Although there are few published studies reporting the efficacy of ECT in the treatment of behavior disorders, character disorders, anxiety neurosis, or feelings of depression related to recently saddening or disappointing events in life, such use has been acceptable in the past to a minority of psychiatrists. Even in children and adolescents, the use of ECT has been acceptable to a small group of psychiatrists on rare and exceptional occasions. If ECT is used in conditions other than the affective disorders and schizophrenia, it is advisable that care be taken to study its effectiveness in a research setting or to seek consultation with colleagues who though understanding the use of ECT generally use a different type of treatment method. No individual is compelled to comply with these suggestions but if we aim to increase knowledge or enrich psychiatric practice by means of an exchange of ideas among the various schools of thought, the measures suggested here are highly desirable.

D. In the absence of the clearly defined conditions listed above in sections A and B, ECT should not be used solely to control symptoms or violent behavior.

E. The idea of selecting ECT as a treatment method for reasons that are politically discriminatory, or for punishment, is abhorrent.

F. Conditions requiring extraordinary care and experience: In the presence of serious physical conditions such as space-occupying intracranial lesions and recent myocardial infarction, as well as advanced pregnancy, the administration of ECT should be in the hands of a team of physicians who, collectively, have had considerable experience both with the use of ECT and with these conditions.

II. Civil Liberties and Informed Consent

The Task Force, recognizing that psychiatric illness can and does at times uniquely modify a patient's capacity to give informed consent, is attempting in these recommendations to balance the individual's clinical needs with his or her civil rights. Particular attention has been paid to this balance because a rigid emphasis on either legal rights or clinical demands leads to poor clinical management. In whichever manner the recommendations regarding consent procedures will be implemented, to be

effective they must ultimately mesh with or be influenced by
local and state regulations and rulings. The following four general categories of patients have been considered in Chapter VII,
pages 143-145. For details, the reader should refer to that section of the report. The categories are: (a) competent patients
who consent to ECT, (b) competent patients who refuse ECT,
(c) incompetent patients incapable of providing informed consent who do not protest the use of ECT in their treatment, and
(d) incompetent or involuntary patients who protest the use of
ECT.

We recommend meticulous record keeping by all psychiatrists and facilities involved in the use of ECT. The records
should include:

  (a) the nature and history of the clinical condition lead-
      ing to the consideration of ECT;
  (b) the details of previous treatments including therapeu-
      tic response and adverse reactions;
  (c) the reasons for selecting ECT;
  (d) the details of all discussions relevant to consent to
      treatment;
  (e) the signed consent form, with the signatures of the
      patient and/or the relatives, or guardian when appro-
      priate;
  (f) the signed concurring and contradictory professional
      opinions where they exist; and
  (g) specifics of the treatment, e.g., unilateral or bilateral
      electrode placement, dates of treatment, characteris-
      tics of the current, drugs administered, etc.

Informed Consent

To provide informed consent, the patient and/or his/her
close relative or guardian must be competent to understand the
following in simple language and, in agreeing, should sign a Consent Form indicating the consent to the procedure:

  (a) the nature and seriousness of the disorder;
  (b) the probable course that is likely with or without
      ECT (without providing guarantees);
  (c) a description of the procedure;

(d) the nature, degree, duration, and probability of significant risks and/or side effects and/or adverse effects. Special attention should be paid to post-treatment confusion and memory dysfunction;

(e) a description of reasonable treatment alternatives,
and why ECT is being recommended.

(f) the right of the patient to accept or refuse ECT, the
right to revoke his/her consent at any time, and acknowledgment that the consent is for a specified
maximum period of time. Additional treatments shall
require a renewed written informed consent; and

(g) the cost of the proposed treatment.

Furthermore, the following information should be entered in
the patient's official record in a standard form;

that the information outlined from (a)-(g) above has been
presented to the patient, and/or his/her relative or
guardian;

that the patient, relative, or guardian is competent to
understand and intelligently act upon this information; and

that the consent for a course of treatment is being provided voluntarily, without coercion.

The above statement should appear before the signature
of the attending physician.

(Those interested in an example of how the information
necessary for informed consent can be presented to patients,
relatives, or guardians should see Appendix I.)

III. The Administration of ECT

Here we wish to emphasize what we have already repeated in
the pages of this document, namely, that what follows is a detailed description of but one of the several methods available
for administering ECT in an acceptable manner. Procedures
which differ in one or more details from that which is described
here are frequently used and may be equally acceptable.

The nature of ECT is such that it should be given with
general anesthesia and muscle relaxation. In view of the safety
and efficacy of these modifications of the procedure and in

view of the discomfort and serious complications that can be associated with an unmodified procedure, the use of unmodified ECT is no longer advised. The setting for the treatment should provide facilities for the modified treatment and for the immediate management of complications that may arise. The treatment team should be competent to deal with routine and special problems and should have facilities for immediate management of complications that may arise.

A. Pre-Treatment Evaluation

This includes an adequate medical and anesthetic history, a thorough physical examination, appropriate laboratory tests, and specialized consultations as indicated. The subject is complicated by the varying pre-anesthetic routines that are customary in the different parts of the country. The Task Force subscribes to the view that the pre-ECT evaluation should embody the principles of good medical practice supplemented by those special procedures, consultations, and investigations relevant to the use of ECT in a particular patient.

The following applies:

(a) The history includes items pertinent to the existence of pulmonary, coronary, vascular, neurological, and orthopedic disease as well as untoward responses to medications, particularly those related to previous anesthetic procedures.

(b) The physical examination includes special attention to the possible existence of pulmonary, coronary, cardiovascular, neurological, and orthopedic disorders. Special attention is paid to the presence of fractured or loose teeth and dental appliances.

(c) Laboratory and special investigations and procedures are considered within the context of the findings of the history and physical examination. Attention is given to a determination of the plasma pseudocholinesterase activity level in selected patients (see Chapter V, page 107) prior to the use of succinylcholine. Spinal radiographic examination is considered in the light of the individual's history and physical examination. X-ray procedures are contraindicated when pregnancy exists, or is possible; [they are] valuable as a means of demonstrating that radiographic abnormalities have existed prior to the proposed treatment (e.g., as a result of a fall, automobile accident, etc.).

The basis for these recommendations and a fuller discussion of the rationale for these and other procedures will be found in Chapter V.

B. Treatment Considerations

It is recommended that:

(a) Precautions be taken so that patients receiving ECT do not have solid materials (e.g., pills, solid food particles) in the stomach because of the danger of regurgitation, vomiting, and possible respiratory tract obstruction.

(b) ECT only be administered in a location, and under circumstances, where there is immediate (i.e., within 2-3 minutes) availability of and access to the professional skills, equipment, and drugs necessary to manage complications which can occur unpredictably whenever the treatment is administered to *any* individual. In general, this will necessitate that the treatment be administered in a hospital or in some appropriately equipped facility.

(c) Whenever possible, the treatment team should include a nurse and aides who have had training and experience in carrying out the procedure of ECT and in managing the complications associated with this form of therapy.

(d) ECT be administered only to patients who are adequately anesthetized, as determined by objective criteria, so that they are unconscious of events during the period prior to the seizure, e.g., discomfort from the succinylcholine muscle contractions, being paralyzed and unable to breathe, and conversations.

(e) An intravenous line (e.g., scalp-vein "butterfly" needle) be maintained, until the patient is responding following the treatment, for the administration of appropriate medications in the event of adverse reactions.

(f) An anticholinergic agent, preferably of the quaternary type (e.g., methscopolamine), be used at the discretion of the physician administering the treatment in doses sufficient to prevent severe bradycardia or asystole during the seizure (see Chapter V).

(g) All patients receive assisted or artificial ventilation with oxygen-enriched gas mixtures from the time that consciousness is lost until a normal tidal volume has been attained at the end of the procedure, except during the convulsion. In patients who are guarded anesthetic-medical risks, a one- or two-minute period of deep breathing of an enriched oxygen mixture before administering the anesthetic agent is recommended as an additional safeguard against hypoxemia and hypercarboxemia.

(h) The individual psychiatrist in each case should decide whether unilateral or bilateral treatment is the best mode of ECT administration for any particular patient. It should be noted that the members of the Task Force have been persuaded by their joint experience and by the available data to favor the use of unilateral ECT because several studies report it to be as effective as bilateral ECT and because memory disability following the unilateral method is considered less than that following bilateral treatment. Nevertheless, some experienced clinicians in the United States currently view unilateral ECT as less effective than bilateral treatment and a few regard it as ineffective. A few of the possible explanations for this disparity between published studies and individual experience are considered in Chapter II, page 21. Further studies of the comparative value of these two methods of administering ECT are strongly recommended.

(i) A technique should be routinely employed to ascertain that a therapeutically adequate seizure has, in fact, been induced. A seizure lasting less than 25 seconds may not be adequate. Three practical methods are available:

(1) observing that a bilateral tonic → clonic progression of muscle convulsive activity has occurred *after* the electrical stimulus has ceased. The tonic contraction

occurring *during* the application of the electrical stimulus is due to the transmotor-cortical passage of the current and does not, in itself, indicate that a therapeutically adequate seizure has been induced.

(2) the "tourniquet" or "controlled convulsion" technique, in which the muscle paralysant is excluded from one extremity by means of an inflated blood pressure cuff, is useful for preserving a mass of unparalyzed muscle which can reliably show the poststimulus tonic → clonic convulsive muscle sequence; or

(3) EEG monitoring of the cerebral seizure.

(j) Psychiatrists recognize that a difference of opinion exists regarding the advisability of glissando and subconvulsive electrical current applications. It is our understanding that memory disability is worsened by increased amounts of electrical current. As both techniques unnecessarily increase the total amount of applied current, we cannot recommend their use although we recognize that they are acceptable techniques to a small minority of psychiatrists. The objective in using them to modify and "soften" or eliminate the convulsion can be more satisfactorily attained by proper use of anesthetic and muscle paralysant drugs.

(k) The teeth should be examined when the convulsion has ceased; appropriate steps should be taken if dental fractures or dislocations have been produced.

(l) Recognition should be accorded the danger associated with the occurrence of regurgitation and/or vomiting at the time skeletal muscle action is reacquired in the immediate post-convulsive period. The danger of pulmonary aspiration is the greatest in the period before pharyngeal and laryngeal reflexes have completely returned. Three precautions will minimize the possibility of pulmonary aspiration:

(1) immediate availability of working suction;

(2) attendants available for immediately turning patient on side; and

(3) particularly in the event that someone is not close by, patient should be placed in prone position until pharyngeal reflexes have definitely returned and until response to verbal statements occurs.

C. Post-Treatment Considerations

It is recommended that:

(a) Adequate supervision should be provided, especially during the period when the patient is drowsy, confused, and less-than-normally alert. This supervision should be directed particularly toward prevention of injury to the patient or to others as a result of:

(1) falling;

(2) operation of motor vehicle or machinery. Outpatients should be sent home in the company of a responsible adult.

(b) During the post-treatment periods, protection should be provided against difficulties in professional, business, work, or personal affairs, as a result of memory dysfunction.

D. General Considerations

It is recommended that:

(a) Scheduling of treatments should be dictated by the nature, severity, and seriousness of the patient's psychiatric disorder, by the presence of associated medical problems, and by the intensity of memory and confusional side effects. Generally, three treatments are given per week. Allowing one or two days between ECTs makes possible a better assessment of the patient's response on a day free of the effects of the treatment.

It may be advisable to administer ECT more frequently, e.g., in severe manic reactions not responsive to drugs or where psychopharmacotherapy entails unacceptable risks. In elderly patients who develop marked memory dysfunction and confusion, once-weekly or twice-weekly treatments may be advisable.

Regarding techniques involving multiple treatments

given under a single anesthetic session (e.g., multiple ECT), the data are inadequate and further study is imperative.

(b) The number of treatments administered to an individual patient should be guided by the following:

affective disorders—Studies of affective disorders suggest that a course of ECT consisting of six to ten treatments is usually sufficient to give satisfactory response on the average case. It is recommended that if an affective disorder has not adequately responded to a course of 15 ECTs, additional treatments should not be administered except under unusual circumstances and after there has been a careful review of the patient's diagnosis, treatment program, and possible alternative forms of therapy. The Task Force recommends that care, judgment, and restraint be exercised before prescribing a second course of ECT within a 12-month period.

psychotic disorders—In the absence of adequate published data regarding the use of ECT in the psychoses (especially the schizophrenias), the Task Force considers it inadvisable to make precise recommendations. Although in many instances a smaller number might suffice, we suggest that the maximum number of ECTs per course not exceed 25-30 treatments. In those exceptional cases where the attending physician believes that a second course is indicated, it is advisable that he/she consult with colleagues before proceeding.

maintenance ECT—Here again the published data regarding this use of ECT are inadequate. Further study and the documentation of clinical data are imperative.

(c) Psychiatrists recognize the lack of consensus regarding the administration of ECT to patients who have, within the previous seven to ten days, been receiving:

reserpine and reserpine-containing preparations;
monoamine oxidase inhibitors;
anticholinesterases;
tricyclic antidepressants;
lithium; or
antipsychotic drugs.

While some authorities believe that psychotropic drugs used in conjunction with ECT may enhance outcome in selected patients, others indicate that since psychotropic drugs have potent venous pooling effects and can cause hypotension, the possible advantage of using them simultaneously with ECT may not be uncomplicated. This issue needs further study.

(d) The so-called reactivation technique should not be employed as a therapeutic measure. This technique requires that the patient be conscious and able to evoke certain thoughts (e.g., depressive ideation) immediately prior to the induction of the seizure. The thesis that this evoked material is particularly susceptible to ECT-induced retrograde amnesia is based on *animal* work which is itself inconclusive and controversial. This fact notwithstanding, the Task Force feels that the use of this technique is incompatible with our recommendation that patients receiving ECT should be rendered unconscious by the use of adequate depths of anesthesia. The reactivation technique is an experimental procedure which should be used only under appropriate investigational conditions (see Section V on Research, this Chapter).

F

●●●●●●●●●●●●●●●●●●●●●●●●●●●●●●●●

American Psychological Association, Ethical Principles of Psychologists

Principle 1: Responsibility

In providing services, psychologists maintain the highest standards of their profession. They accept responsibility for the consequences of their acts and make every effort to insure that their services are used appropriately.

a. As scientists, psychologists accept responsibility for the selection of their research topics and the methods used in investigation, analysis, and reporting. They plan their research in ways to minimize the possibility that their findings will be misleading. They provide thorough discussion of the limitations of their data, especially where their work touches on social policy or might be construed to the detriment of persons in specific age, sex, ethnic, socioeconomic or other social groups. In publishing reports of their work, they never suppress disconfirming data, and they acknowledge the existence of alternative hypotheses and explanations of their findings. Psychologists take credit only for work they have actually done.

b. Psychologists clarify in advance with all appropriate persons and agencies the expectations for sharing and utilizing research data. They avoid relationships which may limit their objectivity or create a conflict of interest. Interference with the milieu in which the data are collected is kept to a minimum.

c. Psychologists have the responsibility to attempt to

American Psychological Association, *Ethical Principles of Psychologists* (Washington, D.C.: American Psychological Association, 1981. Copyright 1981 by the American Psychological Association. Reprinted by permission.

prevent distortion, misuse, or suppression of psychological findings by the institution or agency of which they are employees.

d. As members of governmental or other organizational bodies, psychologists remain accountable as individuals to the highest standards of their profession.

e. As teachers, psychologists recognize their primary obligation to help others acquire knowledge and skill. They maintain high standards of scholarship by presenting psychological information objectively, fully, and accurately.

f. As practitioners, psychologists know that they bear a heavy social responsibility because their recommendations and professional actions may alter the lives of others. They are alert to personal, social, organizational, financial, or political situations and pressures that might lead to misuse of their influence.

Undue Influence

Principle 2: Competence

The maintenance of high standards of competence is a responsibility shared by all psychologists in the interest of the public and the profession as a whole. Psychologists recognize the boundaries of their competence and the limitations of their techniques. They only provide services and only use techniques for which they are qualified by training and experience. In those areas in which recognized standards do not yet exist, psychologists take whatever precautions are necessary to protect the welfare of their clients. They maintain knowledge of current scientific and professional information related to the services they render.

a. Psychologists accurately represent their competence, education, training, and experience. They claim as evidence of educational qualifications only those degrees obtained from institutions acceptable under the Bylaws and Rules of Council of the American Psychological Association.

b. As teachers, psychologists perform their duties on the basis of careful preparation so that their instruction is accurate, current, and scholarly.

c. Psychologists recognize the need for continuing education and are open to new procedures and changes in expectations and values over time.

d. Psychologists recognize differences among people, such as those that may be associated with age, sex, socioeconomic, and ethnic backgrounds. When necessary, they obtain training, experience, or counsel to assure competent service or research relating to such persons.

e. Psychologists responsible for decisions involving individuals or policies based on test results have an understanding of psychological or educational measurement, validation problems, and test research.

f. Psychologists recognize that personal problems and conflicts may interfere with professional effectiveness. Accordingly, they refrain from undertaking any activity in which their personal problems are likely to lead to inadequate performance or harm to a client, colleague, student, or research participant. If engaged in such activity when they become aware of their personal problems, they seek competent professional assistance to determine whether they should suspend, terminate, or limit the scope of their professional and/or scientific activities.

Principle 3: Moral and Legal Standards

Psychologists' moral and ethical standards of behavior are a personal matter to the same degree as they are for any other citizen, except as these may compromise the fulfillment of their professional responsibilities, or reduce the public trust in psychology and psychologists. Regarding their own behavior, psychologists are sensitive to prevailing community standards and to the possible impact that conformity to or deviation from these standards may have upon the quality of their performance as psychologists. Psychologists are also aware of the possible impact of their public behavior upon the ability of colleagues to perform their professional duties.

a. As teachers, psychologists are aware of the fact that their personal values may affect the selection and presentation of instructional materials. When dealing with topics that may give offense, they recognize and respect the diverse attitudes that students may have toward such materials.

b. As employees or employers, psychologists do not engage in or condone practices that are inhumane or that result in illegal or unjustifiable actions. Such practices include but are not limited to those based on considerations of race, handicap, age, gender, sexual preference, religion, or national origin in hiring, promotion, or training.

c. In their professional roles, psychologists avoid any action that will violate or diminish the legal and civil rights of clients or of others who may be affected by their actions.

d. As practitioners and researchers, psychologists act in accord with Association standards and guidelines related to the practice and to the conduct of research with human beings and animals. In the ordinary course of events psychologists adhere to relevant governmental laws and institutional regulations. When federal, state, provincial, organizational, or institutional laws, regulations, or practices are in conflict with Association standards and guidelines, psychologists make known their commitment to Association standards and guidelines, and wherever possible work toward a resolution of the conflict. Both practitioners and researchers are concerned with the development of such legal and quasi-legal regulations as best serve the public interest, and they work toward changing existing regulations that are not beneficial to the public interest.

Principle 4: Public Statements

Public statements, announcements of services, advertising, and promotional activities of psychologists serve the purpose of helping the public make informed judgments and choices. Psychologists represent accurately and objectively their professional qualifications, affiliations, and functions, as well as those of the institutions or organizations with which they or the statements may be associated. In public statements providing psychological information or professional opinions or providing information about the availablity of psychological products, publications, and services, psychologists base their statements on scientifically acceptable psychological findings and techniques with full recognition of the limits and uncertainties of such evidence.

a. When announcing or advertising professional services, psychologists may list the following information to describe the provider and services provided: name, highest relevant academic degree earned from a regionally accredited institution, date, type and level of certification or licensure, diplomate status, APA membership status, address, telephone number, office hours, a brief listing of the type of psychological services offered, an appropriate presentation of fee information, foreign languages spoken, and policy with regard to third-party payments. Additional relevant or important consumer information may be included if not prohibited by other sections of these Ethical Principles.

b. In announcing or advertising the availability of psychological products, publications, or services, psychologists do not present their affiliation with any organization in a manner that falsely implies sponsorship or certification by that organization. In particular and for example, psychologists do not state APA membership or fellow status in a way to suggest that such status implies specialized professional competence or qualifications. Public statements include, but are not limited to, communication by means of periodical, book, list, directory, television, radio, or motion picture. They do not contain: (i) a false, fraudulent, misleading, deceptive, or unfair statement; (ii) a misinterpretation of fact, or a statement likely to mislead or deceive because in context it makes only a partial disclosure of relevant facts; (iii) a testimonial from a patient regarding the quality of a psychologist's services or products; (iv) a statement intended or likely to create false or unjustified expectations of favorable results; (v) a statement implying unusual, unique, or one-of-a-kind abilities; (vi) a statement intended or likely to appeal to a client's fears, anxieties, or emotions concerning the possible results of a failure to obtain the offered services; (vii) a statement concerning the comparative desirability of offered services; (viii) a statement of direct solicitation of individual clients.

Fraud

c. Psychologists do not compensate or give anything of value to a representative of the press, radio, television, or other communication medium in anticipation of or in return for professional publicity in a news item. A paid advertisement must be identified as such, unless it is apparent from the context that it is a paid advertisement. If communicated to the public by use of radio or television, an advertisement shall be prerecorded and approved for broadcast by the psychologist, and a recording of the actual transmission shall be retained by the psychologist.

d. Announcements or advertisements of "personal growth groups," clinics, and agencies give a clear statement of purpose and a clear description of the experiences to be provided. The education, training, and experience of the staff members are appropriately specified.

e. Psychologists associated with the development or promotion of psychological devices, books, or other products offered for commercial sale make reasonable efforts to insure that announcements and advertisements are presented in a professional, scientifically acceptable, and factually informative manner.

f. Psychologists do not participate for personal gain in commercial announcements or advertisements recommending to the public the purchase or use of proprietary or single-source products or services when that participation is based solely upon their identification as psychologists.

g. Psychologists present the science of psychology and offer their services, products, and publications fairly and accurately, avoiding misrepresentation through sensationalism, exaggeration, or superficiality. Psychologists are guided by the primary obligation to aid the public in developing informed judgments, opinions, and choices.

h. As teachers, psychologists insure that statements in catalogs and course outlines are accurate and not misleading, particularly in terms of subject matter to be covered, bases for evaluating progress, and the nature of course experiences. Announcements, brochures, or advertisements describing workshops, seminars, or other educational programs accurately describe the audience for which the program is intended as well as eligibility requirements, educational objectives, and nature of the materials to be covered. These announcements also accurately represent the education, training, and experience of the psychologists presenting the programs, and any fees involved.

i. Public announcements or advertisements soliciting research participants, in which clinical services or other professional services are offered as an inducement, make clear the nature of the services as well as the costs and other obligations to be accepted by the participants of the research.

j. Psychologists accept the obligation to correct others who represent that psychologist's professional qualifications, or associations with products or services, in a manner incompatible with these guidelines.

k. Individual diagnostic and therapeutic services are provided only in the context of a professional psychological relationship. When personal advice is given by means of public lecture or demonstration, newspaper or magazine articles, radio or television programs, mail or similar media, the psychologist utilizes the most current relevant data and exercises the highest level of professional judgment.

l. Products that are described or presented by means of public lectures or demonstrations, newspaper or magazine articles, radio or television programs, or similar media meet the same recognized standards as exist for use in the context of a professional relationship.

Principle 5: Confidentiality

Psychologists have a primary obligation to respect the confidentiality of information obtained from persons in the course of their work as psychologists. They reveal such information to others only with the consent of the person or the person's legal representative, except in those circumstances in which not to do so would result in clear danger to the person or to others. Where appropriate, psychologists inform their clients of the legal limits of confidentiality.

Duty to Warn

Informed Consent

a. Information obtained in clinical or consulting relationships, or evaluative data concerning children, students, employees, and others, are discussed only for professional purposes and only with persons clearly concerned with the case. Written and oral reports present only data germane to the purposes of the evaluation and every effort is made to avoid undue invasion of privacy.

Invasion of Privacy

b. Psychologists who present personal information obtained during the course of professional work in writings, lectures, or other public forums either obtain adequate prior consent to do so or adequately disguise all identifying information.

c. Psychologists make provisions for maintaining confidentiality in the storage and disposal of records.

d. When working with minors or other persons who are unable to give voluntary, informed consent, psychologists take special care to protect these persons' best interests.

Principle 6: Welfare of the Consumer

Psychologists respect the integrity and protect the welfare of the people and groups with whom they work. When there is a conflict of interest between a client and the psychologist's employing institution, psychologists clarify the nature and direction of their loyalties and responsibilities and keep all parties informed of their commitments. Psychologists fully inform consumers as to the purpose and nature of an evaluative, treatment, educational, or training procedure, and they freely acknowledge that clients, students, or participants in research have freedom of choice with regard to participation. *[Informed Consent]*

a. Psychologists are continually cognizant of their own needs and of their potentially influential position vis-à-vis persons such as clients, students, and subordinates. They avoid exploiting the trust and dependency of such persons. Psychologists make every effort to avoid dual relationships which could impair their professional judgment or increase the risk of exploitation. Examples of such dual relationships include but are not limited to research with and treatment of employees, students, supervisees, close friends, or relatives. Sexual intimacies with clients are unethical. *[Undue Influence]*

b. When a psychologist agrees to provide services to a client at the request of a third party, the psychologist assumes the responsibility of clarifying the nature of the relationships to all parties concerned.

c. Where the demands of an organization require psychologists to violate these Ethical Principles, psychologists clarify the nature of the conflict between the demand and these principles. They inform all parties of psychologists' ethical responsibilities, and take appropriate action.

d. Psychologists make advance financial arrangements that safeguard the best interests of and are clearly understood by their clients. They neither give nor receive any remuneration for referring clients for professional services. They contribute a portion of their services to work for which they receive little or no financial return.

Termination   e. Psychologists terminate a clinical or consulting relationship when it is reasonably clear that the consumer is not benefiting from it. They offer to help the consumer locate alternative sources of assistance.

Principle 7: Professional Relationships

Psychologists act with due regard for the needs, special competencies, and obligations of their colleagues in psychology and other professions. They respect the prerogatives and obligations of the institutions or organizations with which these other colleagues are associated.

a. Psychologists understand the areas of competence of related professions. They make full use of all the professional, technical, and administrative resources that serve the best interests of consumers. The absence of formal relationships with other professional workers does not relieve psychologists of the responsibility of securing for their clients the best possible professional services nor does it relieve them of the obligation to exercise foresight, diligence, and tact in obtaining the complementary or alternative assistance needed by clients.

b. Psychologists know and take into account the traditions and practices of other professional groups with whom they work and cooperate fully with such groups. If a person is receiving similar services from another professional, psychologists do not offer their own services directly to such a person. If a psychologist is contacted by a person who is already receiving similar services from another professional, the psychologist carefully considers that professional relationship and proceeds with caution and sensitivity to the therapeutic issues as well as the client's welfare. The psychologist discusses these issues with the client so as to minimize the risk of confusion and conflict.

c. Psychologists who employ or supervise other professionals or professionals in training accept the obligation to facilitate the further professional development of these individuals. They provide appropriate working conditions, timely evaluations, constructive consultation, and experience opportunities.

d. Psychologists do not exploit their professional relationships with clients, supervisees, students, employees, or research participants sexually or otherwise. Psychologists do not condone nor engage in sexual harassment. Sexual harassment is defined as deliberate or repeated comments, gestures, or physical contacts of a sexual nature that are unwanted by the recipient.

Fiduciary Duty

Sex as Innovative Therapy

e. In conducting research in institutions or organizations, psychologists secure appropriate authorization to conduct such research. They are aware of their obligation to future research workers and insure that host institutions receive adequate information about the research and proper acknowledgment of their contributions.

f. Publication credit is assigned to those who have contributed to a publication in proportion to their professional contribution. Major contributions of a professional character made by several persons to a common project are recognized by joint authorship, with the individual who made the principal contribution listed first. Minor contributions of a professional character and extensive clerical or similar nonprofessional assistance may be acknowledged in footnotes or in an introductory statement. Acknowledgment through specific citations is made for unpublished as well as published material that has directly influenced the research or writing. A psychologist who compiles and edits material of others for publication publishes the material in the name of the originating group, if appropriate, with his/her own name appearing as chairperson or editor. All contributors are to be acknowledged and named.

g. When psychologists know of an ethical violation by another psychologist, and it seems appropriate, they informally attempt to resolve the issue by bringing the behavior to the attention of the psychologist. If the misconduct is of a minor nature and/or appears to be due to lack of sensitivity, knowledge, or experience, such an informal solution is usually appropriate. Such informal corrective efforts are sensitive to any rights to confidentiality involved. If the violation does not seem amenable to an informal solution, or is of a more serious nature, psychologists bring it to the attention of the appropriate local, state, and/or national committee on professional ethics and conduct.

Principle 8: Assessment Techniques

In the development, publication, and utilization of psychological assessment techniques, psychologists make every effort to promote the welfare and best interests of the client. They guard against the misuse of assessment results. They respect the client's right to know the results, the interpretations made, and the bases for their conclusions and recommendations. Psychologists make every effort to maintain the security of tests and other assessment techniques within limits of legal mandates. They strive to assure the appropriate use of assessment techniques by others.

Informed Consent

a. In using assessment techniques, psychologists respect the right of clients to have a full explanation of the nature and purpose of the techniques in language that the client can understand, unless an explicit exception to this right has been agreed upon in advance. When the explanations are to be provided by others, the psychologist establishes procedures for insuring the adequacy of these explanations.

b. Psychologists responsible for the development and standardization of psychological tests and other assessment techniques utilize established scientific procedures and observe the relevant APA standards.

Diagnosis

c. In reporting assessment results, psychologists indicate any reservations that exist regarding validity or reliability because of the circumstances of the assessment or the inappropriateness of the norms for the person tested. Psychologists strive to insure that the results of assessments and their interpretations are not misused by others.

d. Psychologists recognize that assessment results may become obsolete. They make every effort to avoid and prevent the misuse of obsolete measures.

e. Psychologists offering scoring and interpretation services are able to produce appropriate evidence for the validity of the programs and procedures used in arriving at interpretations. The public offering of an automated interpretation service is considered as a professional-to-professional consultation. The psychologist makes every effort to avoid misuse of assessment reports.

f. Psychologists do not encourage or promote the use of psychological assessment techniques by inappropriately trained or otherwise unqualified persons through teaching, sponsorship, or supervision.

Principle 9: Research with Human Participants

The decision to undertake research rests upon a considered judgment by the individual psychologist about how best to contribute to psychological science and human welfare. Having made the decision to conduct research, the psychologist considers alternative directions in which research energies and resources might be invested. On the basis of this consideration, the psychologist carries out the investigation with respect and concern for the dignity and welfare of the people who participate, and with cognizance of federal and state regulations and professional standards governing the conduct of research with human participants.

a. In planning a study, the investigator has the responsibility to make a careful evaluation of its ethical acceptability. To the extent that the weighing of scientific and human values suggests a compromise of any principle, the investigator incurs a correspondingly serious obligation to seek ethical advice and to observe stringent safeguards to protect the rights of human participants.

b. Considering whether a participant in a planned study will be a "subject at risk" or a "subject at minimal risk," according to recognized standards, is of primary ethical concern to the investigator.

c. The investigator always retains the responsibility for insuring ethical practice in research. The investigator is also responsible for the ethical treatment of research participants by collaborators, assistants, students, and employees, all of whom, however, incur similar obligations.

d. Except for minimal risk research, the investigator establishes a clear and fair agreement with the research participants, prior to their participation, that clarifies the obligations and responsibilities of each. The investigator has the obligation to honor all promises and commitments included in that agreement. The investigator informs the participant of all aspects of the research that might reasonably be expected to influence willingness to participate, and explains all other aspects of the research about which the participant inquires. Failure to make full disclosure prior to obtaining informed consent requires additional safeguards to protect the welfare and dignity of the research participant. Research with children or participants who have impairments which would limit understanding and/or communication requires special safeguard procedures.

e. Methodological requirements of a study may make the use of concealment or deception necessary. Before conducting such a study, the investigator has a special responsibility to: (i) determine whether the use of such techniques is justified by the study's prospective scientific, educational, or applied value; (ii) determine whether alternative procedures are available that do not utilize concealment or deception; and (iii) insure that the participants are provided with sufficient explanation as soon as possible.

f. The investigator respects the individual's freedom to decline to participate in or to withdraw from the research at any time. The obligation to protect this freedom requires careful thought and consideration when the investigator is in a position of authority or influence over the participant. Such positions of authority include but are not limited to situations when research participation is required as part of employment or when the participant is a student, client, or employee of the investigator.

g. The investigator protects the participants from physical

and mental discomfort, harm, and danger that may arise from research procedures. If risks of such consequences exist, the investigator informs the participant of that fact. Research procedures likely to cause serious or lasting harm to a participant are not used unless the failure to use these procedures might expose the participant to risk of greater harm, or unless the research has great potential benefit and fully informed and voluntary consent is obtained from each participant. The participant should be informed of procedures for contacting the investigator within a reasonable time period following participation should stress, potential harm, or related questions or concerns arise.

h. After the data are collected, the investigator provides the participant with information about the nature of the study and attempts to remove any misconceptions that may have arisen. Where scientific or humane values justify delaying or withholding information, the investigator incurs a special responsibility to monitor the research and to assure that there are no damaging consequences for the participant.

i. Where research procedures result in undesirable consequences for the individual participant, the investigator has the responsibility to detect and remove or correct these consequences, including long-term effects.

j. Information obtained about the research participant during the course of an investigation is confidential unless otherwise agreed upon in advance. When the possibility exists that others may obtain access to such information, this possibility, together with the plans for protecting confidentiality, is explained to the participant as part of the procedure for obtaining informed consent.

Principle 10: Care and Use of Animals

An investigator of animal behavior strives to advance our understanding of basic behavioral principles and/or to contribute to the improvement of human health and welfare. In seeking these ends, the investigator insures the welfare of the animals and treats them humanely. Laws and regulations notwithstanding, the animal's immediate protection depends upon the scientist's own conscience.

a. The acquisition, care, use, and disposal of all animals is in compliance with current federal, state or provincial, and local laws and regulations.

b. A psychologist trained in research methods and experienced in the care of laboratory animals closely supervises all procedures involving animals and is responsible for insuring appropriate consideration of their comfort, health, and humane treatment.

c. Psychologists insure that all individuals using animals under their supervision have received explicit instruction in experimental methods and in the care, maintenance, and handling of the species being used. Responsibilities and activities of individuals participating in a research project are consistent with their respective competencies.

d. Psychologists make every effort to minimize discomfort, illness, and pain to the animals. A procedure subjecting animals to pain, stress, or privation is used only when an alternative procedure is unavailable and the goal is justified by its prospective scientific, educational, or applied value. Surgical procedures are performed under appropriate anesthesia; techniques to avoid infection and minimize pain are followed during and after surgery.

e. When it is appropriate that the animal's life be terminated, it is done rapidly and painlessly.

G

●●●●●●●●●●●●●●●●●●●●●●●●●●●●●●●●●●●●●●

American Psychological Association, Specialty Guidelines for the Delivery of Services by Clinical Psychologists

The Specialty Guidelines that follow are based on the generic *Standards for Providers of Psychological Services* originally adopted by the American Psychological Association (APA) in September 1974 and revised in January 1977. Together with the generic *Standards,* these *Specialty Guidelines* state the official policy of the Association regarding delivery of services by clinical psychologists. Admission to the practice of psychology is regulated by state statute. It is the position of the Association that licensing be based on generic, and not on specialty, qualifications. Specialty guidelines serve the additional purpose of providing potential users and other interested groups with essential information about particular services available from the several specialties in professional psychology.

Professional psychology specialties have evolved from generic practice in psychology and are supported by university training programs. There are now at least four recognized professional specialties—clinical, counseling, school, and industrial/organizational psychology.

The knowledge base in each of these specialty areas has increased, refining the state of the art to the point that a set of uniform specialty guidelines is now possible and desirable. The present Guidelines are intended to educate the public, the profession, and other interested parties regarding specialty professional practices. They are also intended to facilitate the continued systematic development of the profession.

The content of each Specialty Guideline reflects a consensus of university faculty and public and private practitioners regarding the knowledge base, services provided, problems addressed, and clients served.

Traditionally, all learned disciplines have treated the designation of specialty practice as a reflection of preparation in greater depth in a particular subject matter, together with a voluntary limiting of focus to a more restricted area of practice by the professional. Lack of specialty designation does not preclude general providers of psychological services from using the methods or dealing with the populations of any specialty, except insofar as psychologists voluntarily refrain from providing services that they are not trained to render. It is the intent of these Guidelines, however, that, following the grandparenting period, psychologists will not put themselves forward as *specialists* in a given area of practice unless they meet the qualifications noted in the Guidelines (see Definitions). Therefore, these Guidelines are intended to apply only to those psychologists who voluntarily wish to be designated as *clinical psychologists.* They do not apply to other psychologists.

These Guidelines represent the profession's best judgment of the conditions, credentials, and experience that contribute to competent professional practice. The APA strongly encourages, and plans to participate in, efforts to identify professional practitioner behaviors and job functions, and to validate the relation between these and desired client outcomes. Thus, future revisions of these Guidelines will increasingly reflect the results of such efforts.

These Guidelines follow the format and, wherever applicable, the wording of the generic Standards. The intent of these Guidelines is to improve the quality, effectiveness, and accessibility of psychological services. They are meant to provide guidance to providers, users, and sanctioners with respect to the best judgment of the profession on these matters. Although the Specialty Guidelines have been derived from and are consistent with the generic Standards, they may be used as a separate document. However, *Standards for Providers of Psychological Services* shall remain the basic policy statement and shall take precedence where there are questions of interpretation.

Professional psychology in general and clinical psychology as a specialty have labored long and diligently to codify a uniform set of guidelines for the delivery of services by clinical psychologists that would serve the respective needs of users, providers, third-party purchasers, and sanctioners of psychological services.

The Committee on Professional Standards established by the APA in January 1980 is charged with keeping the generic Standards and the Specialty Guidelines responsive to the needs of the public and the profession. It also is charged continually to review, modify, and extend them progressively as the profession and the science of psychology develop new knowledge, improved methods, and additional modes of psychological services.

The Specialty Guidelines that follow, for the delivery of services by clinical psychologists, have been established by the APA as a means of self-regulation to protect the public interest. They guide the specialty practice of clinical psychology by specifying important areas of quality assurance and performance that contribute to the goal of facilitating more effective human functioning.

Principles and Implications of Specialty Guidelines

These Guidelines have emerged from and reaffirm the same basic principles that guided the development of the generic *Standards for Providers of Psychological Services*:

1. These Guidelines recognize that admission to the practice of psychology is regulated by state statute.

2. It is the intention of the APA that the generic Standards provide appropriate guidelines for statutory licensing of psychologists. In addition, although it is the position of the APA that licensing be generic and not in specialty areas, these Specialty Guidelines in clinical psychology provide an authoritative reference for use in credentialing specialty providers of

clinical psychological services by such groups as divisions of the
APA and state associations, and by boards and agencies that
find such criteria useful for quality assurance.

3. A uniform set of Specialty Guidelines governs the
quality of services to all users of clinical psychological services
in both the private and the public sectors. Those receiving clinical psychological services are protected by the same kinds of
safeguards, irrespective of sector; these include constitutional
guarantees, statutory regulation, peer review, consultation, record review, and supervision.

4. A uniform set of Specialty Guidelines governs clinical
psychological service functions offered by clinical psychologists, regardless of setting or form of remuneration. All clinical
psychologists in professional practice recognize and are responsive to a uniform set of Specialty Guidelines, just as they are
guided by a common code of ethics.

5. Clinical psychological Guidelines establish clearly
articulated levels of quality for covered clinical psychological
service functions, regardless of the character of the users, purchasers, or sanctioners of such covered services.

6. All persons providing clinical psychological services
meet specified levels of training and experience that are consistent with, and appropriate to, the functions they perform. Clinical psychological services provided by persons who do not meet
the APA qualifications for a professional clinical psychologist
(see Definitions) are supervised by a professional clinical psychologist. Final responsibility and accountability for services
provided rest with professional clinical psychologists.

7. When providing any of the covered clinical psychological service functions at any time and in any setting, whether
public or private, profit or nonprofit, clinical psychologists observe these Guidelines in order to promote the best interests and
welfare of the users of such services. The extent to which clinical psychologists observe these Guidelines is judged by peers.

8. These Guidelines, while assuring the user of the clinical psychologist's accountability for the nature and quality of
services specified in this document, do not preclude the clinical
psychologist from using new methods or developing innovative
procedures in the delivery of clinical services.

These Specialty Guidelines have broad implications both for users of clinical psychological services and for providers of such services:

1. Guidelines for clinical psychological services provide a foundation for mutual understanding between provider and user and facilitate more effective evaluation of services provided and outcomes achieved.

2. Guidelines for clinical psychologists are essential for uniformity in specialty credentialing of clinical psychologists.

3. Guidelines give specific content to the profession's concept of ethical practice as it applies to the functions of clinical psychologists.

4. Guidelines for clinical psychological services may have significant impact on tomorrow's education and training models for both professional and support personnel in clinical psychology.

5. Guidelines for the provision of clinical psychological services in human service facilities influence the determination of acceptable structure, budgeting, and staffing patterns in these facilities.

6. Guidelines for clinical psychological services require continual review and revision.

The Guidelines here presented are intended to improve the quality and delivery of clinical psychological services by specifying criteria for key aspects of the practice setting. Some settings may require additional and/or more stringent criteria for specific areas of service delivery.

Systematically applied, these Guidelines serve to establish a more effective and consistent basis for evaluating the performance of individual service providers as well as to guide the organization of clinical psychological service units in human service settings.

Definitions

Providers of clinical psychological services refers to two categories of persons who provide clinical psychological services:

A. Professional clinical psychologists. Professional clinical psychologists have a doctoral degree from a regionally accredited university or professional school providing an organized, sequential clinical psychology program in a department of psychology in a university or college, or in an appropriate department or unit of a professional school. Clinical psychology programs that are accredited by the American Psychological Association are recognized as meeting the definition of a clinical psychology program. Clinical psychology programs that are not accredited by the American Psychological Association meet the definition of a clinical psychology program if they satisfy the following criteria:

1. The program is primarily psychological in nature and stands as a recognizable, coherent organizational entity within the institution.

2. The program provides an integrated, organized sequence of study.

3. The program has an identifiable body of students who are matriculated in that program for a degree.

4. There is a clear authority with primary responsibility for the core and specialty areas, whether or not the program cuts across administrative lines.

5. There is an identifiable psychology faculty, and a psychologist is responsible for the program.

In addition to a doctoral education, clinical psychologists acquire doctoral and postdoctoral training. Patterns of education and training in clinical psychology are consistent with the functions to be performed and the services to be provided, in accordance with the ages, populations, and problems encountered in various settings.

B. All other persons who are not professional clinical psychologists and who participate in the delivery of clinical psychological services under the supervision of a professional clinical psychologist. Although there may be variations in the titles of such persons, they are not referred to as clinical psychologists. Their functions may be indicated by use of the adjective *psychological* preceding the noun, for example, *psychological associate, psychological assistant, psychological technician,* or *psychological aide.* Their services are rendered under the supervision of a professional clinical psychologist, who is responsible for the designation given them and for quality control. To be assigned such a designation, a person has the background, training, or experience that is appropriate to the functions performed.

Clinical psychological services refers to the application of principles, methods, and procedures for understanding, predicting, and alleviating intellectual, emotional, psychological, and behavioral disability and discomfort. Direct services are provided in a variety of health settings, and direct and supportive services are provided in the entire range of social, organizational, and academic institutions and agencies. Clinical psychological services include the following:

A. Assessment directed toward diagnosing the nature and causes, and predicting the effects, of subjective distress; of personal, social, and work dysfunction; and of the psychological and emotional factors involved in, and consequent to, physical disease and disability. Procedures may include, but are not limited to, interviewing, and administering and interpreting tests of intellectual abilities, attitudes, emotions, motivations, personality characteristics, psychoneurological status, and other aspects of human experience and behavior relevant to the disturbance.

B. Interventions directed at identifying and correcting the emotional conflicts, personality disturbances, and skill deficits underlying a person's distress and/or dysfunction. Interventions may reflect a variety of theoretical orientations, techniques, and modalities. These may include, but are not limited to, psychotherapy, psychoanalysis, behavior therapy, marital and family therapy, group psychotherapy, hypnotherapy, social-learning approaches, biofeedback techniques, and environmental consultation and design.

C. Professional consultation in relation to A and B above.

D. Program development services in the areas of A, B, and C above.

E. Supervision of clinical psychological services.

F. Evaluation of all services noted in A through E above.

A *clinical psychological service unit* is the functional unit through which clinical psychological services are provided; such a unit may be part of a larger psychological service organization comprising psychologists of more than one specialty and headed by a professional psychologist.

A. A clinical psychological service unit provides predominantly clinical psychological services and is composed of one or more professional clinical psychologists and supporting staff.

B. A clinical psychological service unit may operate as a professional service or as a functional or geographic component of a larger multipsychological service unit or of a governmental, educational, correctional, health, training, industrial, or commercial organizational unit.

C. One or more clinical psychologists providing professional services in a multidisciplinary setting constitute a clinical psychological service unit.

D. A clinical psychological service unit may also be one or more clinical psychologists in a private practice or a psychological consulting firm.

Users of clinical psychological services include:

A. Direct users or recipients of clinical psychological services.

B. Public and private institutions, facilities, or organizations receiving clinical psychological services.

C. Third-party purchasers—those who pay for the delivery of services but who are not the recipients of services.

D. Sanctioners—those who have a legitimate concern with the accessibility, timeliness, efficacy, and standards of quality attending the provision of clinical psychological services. Sanctioners may include members of the user's family, the court, the probation officer, the school administrator, the employer, the union representative, the facility director, etc. Sanctioners may also include various governmental, peer-review, and accreditation bodies concerned with the assurance of quality.

Guideline 1. Providers

1.1 Each clinical psychological service unit offering psychological services has available at least one professional clinical psychologist and as many more professional clinical psychologists as are necessary to assure the adequacy and quality of services offered.

INTERPRETATION: The intent of this Guideline is that one or more providers of psychological services in any clinical psychological service unit meet the levels of training and experience of the professional clinical psychologist as specified in the preceding definitions.

When a facility offering clinical psychological services does not have a full-time professional clinical psychologist available, the facility retains the services of one or more professional clinical psychologists on a regular part-time basis. The clinical psychologist so retained directs and supervises the psychological services provided, participates sufficiently to be able to assess the need for services, reviews the content of services provided, and has the authority to assume professional responsibility and accountability for them.

The psychologist directing the service unit is responsible for determining and justifying appropriate ratios of psychologists to users and psychologists to support staff, in order to assure proper scope, accessibility, and quality of services provided in that setting.

1.2 Providers of clinical psychological services who do not meet the requirements for the professional clinical psychologist are supervised directly by a professional clinical psychologist who assumes professional responsibility and accountability for the services provided. The level and extent of supervision may vary from task to task so long as the supervising psychologist retains a sufficiently close supervisory relationship to meet this Guideline. Special proficiency training or supervision may be provided by a professional psychologist of another specialty or by a professional from another discipline whose competence in the given area has been demonstrated by previous training and experience.

INTERPRETATION: In each clinical psychological service unit there may be varying levels of responsibility with respect to the nature and quality of services provided. Support personnel are considered to be responsible for their functions and behavior when assisting in the provision of clinical psychological service and are accountable to the professional clinical psychologist. Ultimate professional responsibility and accountability for the services provided require that the supervisor review and

Supervision

approve reports and test protocols, review and approve intervention plans and strategies, and review outcomes. Therefore, the supervision of all clinical psychological services is provided directly by a professional clinical psychologist in individual and/or group face-to-face meetings.

In order to meet this Guideline, an appropriate number of hours per week are devoted to direct face-to-face supervision of each clinical psychological service unit staff member. In no event is it less than 1 hour per week of such supervision. The more comprehensive the psychological services are, the more supervision will be needed. A plan or formula for relating increasing amounts of supervisory time to the complexity of professional responsibilities is to be developed. The amount and nature of supervision is made known to all parties concerned.

Such communications are in writing and describe and delineate the duties of the employee with respect to range and type of services to be provided. The limits of independent action and decision making are defined. The description of responsibility also specifies the means by which the employee will contact the professional clinical psychologist in the event of emergency or crisis situations.

1.3 Wherever a clinical psychological service unit exists, a professional clinical psychologist is responsible for planning, directing, and reviewing the provision of clinical psychological services. Whenever the clinical psychological service unit is part of a larger professional psychological service encompassing various psychological specialties, a professional psychologist is the administrative head of the service.

INTERPRETATION: The clinical psychologist coordinates the activities of the clinical psychological service unit with other professional, administrative, and technical groups, both within and outside the facility. This clinical psychologist, who may be the director, chief, or coordinator of the clinical psychological service unit, has related responsibilities including, but not limited to, recruiting qualified staff, directing training and research activities of the service, maintaining a high level of professional and ethical practice, and ensuring that staff members function only within the areas of their competency.

In order to facilitate the effectiveness of clinical services by raising the level of staff sensitivity and professional skills, the clinical psychologist designated as director is responsible for participating in the selection of the staff and support personnel whose qualifications and skills (e.g., language, cultural and experiential background, race, sex, and age) are directly relevant to the needs and characteristics of the users served.

1.4 When functioning as part of an organizational setting, professional clinical psychologists bring their backgrounds and skills to bear on the goals of the organization, whenever appropriate, by participation in the planning and development of overall services.

INTERPRETATION: Professional clinical psychologists participate in the maintenance of high professional standards by representation on committees concerned with service delivery.

As appropriate to the setting, their activities may include active participation, as voting and as office-holding members, on the professional staffs of hospitals and other facilities, and on other executive, planning, and evaluation boards and committees.

1.5 Clinical psychologists maintain current knowledge of scientific and professional developments to maintain and enhance their professional competence.

INTERPRETATION: Methods through which knowledge of scientific and professional development may be gained include, but are not limited to, reading scientific and professional publications, attendance at workshops, participation in staff development programs, and other forms of continuing education. The clinical psychologist has ready access to reference material related to the provision of psychological services. Clinical psychologists are prepared to show evidence periodically that they are staying abreast of current knowledge and practices in the field of clinical psychology through continuing education.

1.6 Clinical psychologists limit their practice to their demonstrated areas of professional competence.

INTERPRETATION: Clinical psychological services are offered in accordance with the providers' areas of competence as defined by verifiable training and experience. When extending services beyond the range of their usual practice, psychologists obtain pertinent training or appropriate professional supervision. Such training or supervision is consistent with the extension of functions performed and services provided. An extension of services may involve a change in the theoretical orientation of the clinical psychologist, a change in modality or technique, or a change in the type of client and/or the kinds of problems or disorders for which services are to be provided (e.g., children, elderly persons, mental retardation, neurological impairment).

1.7 Professional psychologists who wish to qualify as clinical psychologists meet the same requirements with respect to subject matter and professional skills that apply to doctoral and postdoctoral education and training in clinical psychology.

INTERPRETATION: Education of doctoral-level psychologists to qualify them for specialty practice in clinical psychology is under the auspices of a department in a regionally accredited university or of a professional school that offers the doctoral degree in clinical psychology. Such education is individualized, with due credit given for relevant coursework and other requirements that have been satisfied previously. In addition, doctoral-level training plus 1 year of postdoctoral experience supervised by a clinical psychologist is required. Merely taking an internship in clinical psychology or acquiring experience in a practicum setting is not adequate preparation for becoming a clinical psychologist when prior education has not been in that area. Fulfillment of such an individualized educational program is attested to by the awarding of a certificate by the supervising department or professional school, indicating the successful completion of preparation in clinical psychology.

1.8 Professional clinical psychologists are encouraged to develop innovative theories and procedures and to provide appropriate theoretical and/or empirical support for their innovations.

INTERPRETATION: A specialty of a profession rooted in

a science intends continually to explore and experiment with a view to developing and verifying new and improved methods of serving the public in ways that can be documented.

Guideline 2. Programs

2.1 Composition and organization of a clinical psychological
    service unit:
    2.1.1 The composition and programs of a clinical psycho-
          logical service unit are responsive to the needs of the
          persons or settings served.

INTERPRETATION: A clinical psychological service unit is structured so as to facilitate effective and economical delivery of services. For example, a clinical psychological service unit serving a predominantly low-income, ethnic, or racial minority group has a staffing pattern and service programs that are adapted to the linguistic, experiential, and attitudinal characteristics of the users.

    2.1.2 A description of the organization of the clinical psy-
          chological service unit and its lines of responsibility
          and accountability for the delivery of psychological
          services is available in written form to staff of the
          unit and to users and sanctioners upon request.

INTERPRETATION: The description includes lines of responsibility, supervisory relationships, and the level and extent of accountability for each person who provides psychological services.

    2.1.3 A clinical psychological service unit includes suffi-
          cient numbers of professional and support personnel
          to achieve its goals, objectives, and purposes.

INTERPRETATION: The workload and diversity of psychological services required and the specific goals and objectives of the setting determine the numbers and qualifications of professional and support personnel in the clinical psychological service unit. Where shortages in personnel exist so that psychological services cannot be rendered in a professional manner, the

director of the clinical psychological service unit initiates action to remedy such shortages. When this fails, the director
appropriately modifies the scope or workload of the unit to
maintain the quality of the services rendered.

2.2 Policies:
    2.2.1 When the clinical psychological services unit is com-
         posed of more than one person or is a component of
         a larger organization, a written statement of its ob-
         jectives and scope of services is developed, main-
         tained, and reviewed.

INTERPRETATION: The clinical psychological service unit
reviews its objectives and scope of services annually and revises
them as necessary to ensure that the psychological services offered are consistent with staff competencies and current psychological knowledge and practice. This statement is discussed
with staff, reviewed with the appropriate administrator, and dis-
tributed to users and sanctioners upon request, whenever appropriate.

    2.2.2 All providers within a clinical psychological service
         unit support the legal and civil rights of the users.

INTERPRETATION: Providers of clinical psychological
services safeguard the interests of the users with regard to personal, legal, and civil rights. They are continually sensitive to
the issue of confidentiality of information, the short-term and
long-term impacts of their decisions and recommendations, and
other matters pertaining to individual, legal, and civil rights.
Concerns regarding the safeguarding of individual rights of users
include, but are not limited to, problems of self-incrimination in
judicial proceedings, involuntary commitment to hospitals, protection of minors or legal incompetents, discriminatory practices
in employment selection procedures, recommendation for special education provisions, information relative to adverse personnel actions in the armed services, and the adjudication of domestic relations disputes in divorce and custodial proceedings.
Providers of clinical psychological services take affirmative action by making themselves available for local committees, review

boards, and similar advisory groups established to safeguard the human, civil, and legal rights of service users.

    2.2.3 All providers within a clinical psychological service unit are familiar with and adhere to the American Psychological Association's *Standards for Providers of Psychological Services, Ethical Standards of Psychologists, Standards for Educational and Psychological Tests, Ethical Principles in the Conduct of Research with Human Participants,* and other official policy statements relevant to standards for professional services issued by the Association.

INTERPRETATION: Providers of clinical psychological services maintain up-to-date knowledge of the relevant standards of the American Psychological Association.

    2.2.4 All providers within a clinical psychological service unit conform to relevant statutes established by federal, state, and local governments.

INTERPRETATION: All providers of clinical psychological services are familiar with appropriate statutes regulating the practice of psychology. They observe agency regulations that have the force of law and that relate to the delivery of psychological services (e.g., evaluation for disability retirement and special education placements). In addition, all providers are cognizant that federal agencies such as the Veterans Administration, the Department of Education, and the Department of Health and Human Services have policy statements regarding psychological services, and, where relevant, providers conform to them. Providers of clinical psychological services are also familiar with other statutes and regulations, including those addressed to the civil and legal rights of users (e.g., those promulgated by the federal Equal Employment Opportunity Commission), that are pertinent to their scope of practice.

    It is the responsibility of the American Psychological Association to maintain current files of those federal policies, statutes, and regulations relating to this section and to assist its members in obtaining them. The state psychological associations and the state licensing boards periodically publish and distribute appropriate state statutes and regulations.

> 2.2.5 All providers within a clinical psychological service unit inform themselves about and use the network of human services in their communities in order to link users with relevant services and resources.

INTERPRETATION: Clinical psychologists and support staff are sensitive to the broader context of human needs. In recognizing the matrix of personal and societal problems, providers make available to users information regarding human services such as legal aid societies, social services, employment agencies, health resources, and educational and recreational facilities. Providers of clinical psychological services refer to such community resources and, when indicated, actively intervene on behalf of the users.

Community resources include the private as well as the public sectors. Private resources include private agencies and centers and psychologists in independent private practice. Consultation is sought or referral made within the public or private network of services whenever required in the best interest of the users. Clinical psychologists, in either the private or public setting, utilize other resources in the community whenever indicated because of limitations within the psychological service unit providing the services. Professional clinical psychologists in private practice are familiar with the types of services offered through local community mental health clinics and centers, including alternatives to hospitalization, and know the costs and eligibility requirements for those services.

Consul-
tation

> 2.2.6 In the delivery of clinical psychological services, the providers maintain a cooperative relationship with colleagues and co-workers in the best interest of the users.

INTERPRETATION: Clinical psychologists recognize the areas of special competence of other professional psychologists and of professionals in other fields for either consultation or referral purposes. Providers of clinical psychological services make appropriate use of other professional, research, technical, and administrative resources to serve the best interests of users, and establish and maintain cooperative arrangements with such other resources as are required to meet the needs of users.

2.3 Procedures:

2.3.1 Each clinical psychological service unit follows a set of procedural guidelines for the delivery of psychological services.

INTERPRETATION: Providers are prepared to provide a statement of procedural guidelines, in either oral or written form, in terms that can be understood by users, including sanctioners and local administrators. This statement describes the current methods, forms, procedures, and techniques being used to achieve the objectives and goals for psychological services.

2.3.2 Providers of clinical psychological services develop plans appropriate to the providers' professional practices and to the problems presented by the users.

INTERPRETATION: A clinical psychologist develops a plan that describes the psychological services, their objectives, and the manner in which they will be provided. This plan is in written form; it serves as a basis for obtaining understanding and concurrence from the user and provides a mechanism for subsequent peer review. This plan is, of course, modified as new needs or information develop. *Informed Consent*

A clinical psychologist who provides services as one member of a collaborative effort participates in the development and implementation of the overall service plan and provides for its periodic review.

2.3.3 Accurate, current, and pertinent documentation of essential clinical psychological services provided is maintained.

INTERPRETATION: Records kept of clinical psychological services may include, but are not limited to, identifying data, dates of services, types of services, significant actions taken, and outcome at termination. Providers of clinical psycho- *Records* logical services ensure that essential information concerning services rendered is appropriately recorded within a reasonable time following their completion.

2.3.4 Each clinical psychological service unit follows an established record retention and disposition policy.

INTERPRETATION: The policy on record retention and disposition conforms to federal or state statutes or administrative regulations where such are applicable. In the absence of such regulations, the policy is (a) that the full record be retained intact for 3 years after the completion of planned services or after the date of last contact with the user, whichever is later; (b) that a full record or summary of the record be maintained for an additional 12 years; and (c) that the record may be disposed of no sooner than 15 years after the completion of planned services or after the date of the last contact, whichever is later. These temporal guides are consistent with procedures currently in use by federal record centers.

Statute of Limitations

In the event of the death or incapacity of a clinical psychologst in independent practice, special procedures are necessary to assure the continuity of active services to users and the proper safeguarding of inactive records being retained to meet this Guideline. Following approval by the affected user, it would be appropriate for another clinical psychologist, acting under the auspices of the local Professional Standards Review Committee (PSRC), to review the records with the user and recommend a course of action for continuing professional service, if needed. Depending on local circumstances, the reviewing psychologist may also recommend appropriate arrangements for the balance of the record retention and disposition period.

This Guideline has been designed to meet a variety of circumstances that may arise, often years after a set of psychological services have been completed. More and more records are being utilized in forensic matters, for peer review, and in response to requests from users, other professionals, or other legitimate parties requiring accurate information about the exact dates, nature, course, and outcome of a set of psychological services. These record retention procedures also will provide valuable baseline data for the original psychologist-provider when a previous user returns for additional services.

2.3.5 Providers of clinical psychological services maintain a system to protect confidentiality of their records.

INTERPRETATION: Clinical psychologists are responsible for maintaining the confidentiality of information about users of services, from whatever source derived. All persons supervised by clinical psychologists, including nonprofessional personnel and students, who have access to records of psychological services are required to maintain this confidentiality as a condition of employment.

The clinical psychologist does not release confidential information, except with the written consent of the user directly involved or his or her legal representative. Even after consent for release has been obtained, the clinical psychologist clearly identifies such information as confidential to the recipient of the information. If directed otherwise by statute or regulation with the force of law or by court order, the psychologist may seek a resolution to the conflict that is both ethically and legally feasible and appropriate.

Users are informed in advance of any limits in the setting for maintenance of confidentiality of psychological information. For instance, clinical psychologists in hospital, clinic, or agency settings inform their patients that psychological information in a patient's clinical record may be available without the patient's written consent to other members of the professional staff associated with the patient's treatment or rehabilitation. Similar limitations on confidentiality of psychological information may be present in certain school, industrial, military, or other institutional settings, or in instances where the user has waived confidentiality for purposes of third-party payment.

Informed Consent

Users have the right to obtain information from their psychological records. However, the records are the property of the psychologist or the facility in which the psychologist works and are, therefore, the responsibility of the psychologist and subject to his or her control.

When the user's intention to waive confidentiality is judged by the professional clinical psychologist to be contrary to the user's best interests, or in conflict with the user's civil and legal rights, it is the responsibility of the clinical psychologist to discuss the implications of releasing psychological information, and to assist the user in limiting disclosure only to information required by the present circumstance.

Raw psychological data (e.g., questionnaire returns or test protocols) in which a user is identified are released only with the written consent of the user or his or her legal representative and released only to a person recognized by the clinical psychologist as qualified and competent to use the data.

Any use made of psychological reports, records, or data for research or training purposes is consistent with this Guideline. Additionally, providers of clinical psychological services comply with statutory confidentiality requirements and those embodied in the American Psychological Association's *Ethical Standards of Psychologists.*

Providers of clinical psychological services remain sensitive to both the benefits and the possible misuse of information regarding individuals that is stored in large computerized data banks. Providers use their influence to ensure that such information is used in a socially responsible manner.

Guideline 3. Accountability

3.1 The clinical psychologist's professional activity is guided primarily by the principle of promoting human welfare.

INTERPRETATION: Clinical psychologists provide services to users in a manner that is considerate, effective, economical, and humane. Clinical psychologists make their services readily accessible to users in a manner that facilitates the users' freedom of choice.

Clinical psychologists are mindful of their accountability to the sanctioners of clinical psychological services and to the general public, provided that appropriate steps are taken to protect the confidentiality of the service relationship. In the pursuit of their professional activities, they aid in the conservation of human, material, and financial resources.

The clinical psychological service unit does not withhold services to a potential client on the basis of that user's race, color, religion, gender, sexual orientation, age, or national origin. Recognition is given, however, to the following considerations: the professional right of clinical psychologists to limit their practice to a specific category of users (e.g., children, adolescents, women); the right and responsibility of clinical psychologists to withhold an assessment procedure when not validly applicable; and the right and responsibility of clinical psychologists to withhold evaluative, psychotherapeutic, counseling, or other services in specific instances where their own limitations or client characteristics might impair the effectiveness of the relationship. Clinical psychologists seek to ameliorate through peer review, consultation, or other personal therapeutic procedures those factors that inhibit the provision of services to particular users. When indicated services are not available, clinical psychologists shall take whatever action is appropriate to inform responsible persons and agencies of the lack of such services.

Clinical psychologists who find that psychological services are being provided in a manner that is discriminatory or exploitative to users and/or contrary to these Guidelines or to state or federal statutes take appropriate corrective action, which may include the refusal to provide services. When conflicts of interest arise, the clinical psychologist is guided in the resolution of differences by the principles set forth in the American Psychological Association's *Ethical Standards of Psychologists* and "Guidelines for Conditions of Employment of Psychologists."

3.2 Clinical psychologists pursue their activities as members of the independent, autonomous profession of psychology.

INTERPRETATION: Clinical psychologists, as members of an independent profession, are responsible both to the public and to their peers through established review mechanisms. Clinical psychologists are aware of the implications of their activities for the profession as a whole. They seek to eliminate discriminatory practices instituted for self-serving purposes that are not in the interest of the users (e.g., arbitrary requirements for referral and supervision by another profession). They are cognizant of their responsibilities for the development of the profession. They participate where possible in the training and career development of students and other providers, participate as appropriate in the training of paraprofessionals or other professionals, and integrate and supervise the implementation of their contributions within the structure established for delivering psychological services. Clinical psychologists facilitate the development of, and participate in, professional standards review mechanisms.

Clinical psychologists seek to work with other professionals in a cooperative manner for the good of the users and the benefit of the general public. Clinical psychologists associated with multidisciplinary settings support the principle that members of each participating profession have equal rights and opportunities to share all privileges and responsibilities of full membership in hospital facilities or other human service facilities and to administer service programs in their respective areas of competence.

3.3 There are periodic, systematic, and effective evaluations of clinical psychological services.

INTERPRETATION: When the clinical psychological service unit is a component of a larger organization, regular evaluation of progress in achieving goals is provided for in the service delivery plan, including consideration of the effectiveness of clinical psychological services relative to costs in terms of use of time and money and the availability of professional and support personnel.

Evaluation of the clinical psychological service delivery system is conducted internally and, when possible, under independent auspices as well. This evaluation includes an assessment of effectiveness (to determine what the service unit accomplished), efficiency (to determine the total costs of providing the service), continuity (to assure that the services are appropriately linked to other human services), availability (to determine appropriate levels and distribution of services and manpower), accessibility (to assure that the services are barrier free to users), and adequacy (to determine whether the services meet the identified needs for such services).

There is a periodic reexamination of review mechanisms to ensure that these attempts at public safeguards are effective and cost efficient and do not place unnecessary encumbrances on the providers or impose unnecessary additional expenses on users or sanctioners for services rendered.

3.4 Clinical psychologists are accountable for all aspects of the services they provide and are responsive to those concerned with these services.

INTERPRETATION: In recognizing their responsibilities to users, and where appropriate and consistent with the users' legal rights and privileged communications, clinical psychologists make available information about, and provide opportunity to participate in, decisions concerning such issues as initiation, termination, continuation, modification, and evaluation of clinical psychological services.

Depending on the settings, accurate and full information is made available to prospective individual or organizational users regarding the qualifications of providers, the nature and extent of services offered and, where appropriate, financial and social costs.

Where appropriate, clinical psychologists inform users of their payment policies and their willingness to assist in obtaining reimbursement. Those who accept reimbursement from a third party are acquainted with the appropriate statutes and regulations and assist their users to understand procedures for submitting claims and limits on confidentiality of claims information, in accordance with pertinent statutes.

Guideline 4. Environment

4.1 Providers of clinical psychological services promote the development in the service setting of a physical, organizational, and social environment that facilitates optimal human functioning.

INTERPRETATION: Federal, state, and local requirements for safety, health, and sanitation are observed.

As providers of services, clinical psychologists are concerned with the environment of their service unit, especially as it affects the quality of service, but also as it impinges on human functioning in the larger unit or organization when the service unit is included in such a larger context. Physical arrangements and organizational policies and procedures are conducive to the human dignity, self-respect, and optimal functioning of users, and to the effective delivery of service. Attention is given to the comfort and the privacy of users. The atmosphere in which clinical psychological services are rendered is appropriate to the service and to the users, whether in office, clinic, school, industrial organization, or other institutional setting.

Bibliography

Adams, H., and Orgel, R. *Through the Mental Health Maze: A Consumer's Guide to Finding a Psychotherapist.* Washington, D.C.: Health Research Group, 1975.

Andrade, P. D., and Andrade, J. C. "Professional Liability of the Psychiatric Nurse." *Journal of Psychiatry and Law,* 1979, *7* (2), 141-186.

Appleton, W. S. "Legal Problems in Psychiatric Drug Prescription." *American Journal of Psychiatry,* 1968, *124,* 877-882.

Appleton, W. S. "Psychotherapist Prescribes a Drug in His Office: Medicolegal Risks." *Medical Trial Technique Quarterly,* 1970, *17,* 207-216.

Arons, B. S. "Working in the Cuckoo's Nest: An Essay on Present Changes in Mental Health Law and the Changing Role of Psychiatrists in Relation to Patient and Society." *Toledo Law Review,* 1977, *9,* 73-93.

Ayers, R. J., and Holbrook, J. T. "Law, Psychotherapy, and the Duty to Warn: A Tragic Trilogy." *Baylor Law Review,* 1975, *27,* 677-705.

Bellamy, W. A. "Malpractice Risks Confronting the Psychiatrist: A Nationwide Fifteen-Year Study of Appellate Court Cases, 1946-1961." *American Journal of Psychiatry,* 1962, *119* (3), 769-780.

Bellamy, W. A. "Malpractice in Psychiatry." *Diseases of the Nervous System,* 1965, *5,* 312-320.

Benesohn, H. S., and Resnik, H. L. "Guidelines for 'Suicide Proofing' a Psychiatric Unit." *American Journal of Psychotherapy*, 1973, *27*, 204-212.

Beresford, H. R. "Legal Issues Relating to Electroconvulsive Therapy." *Archives of General Psychiatry*, 1971, *25* (8), 100-102.

Beresford, H. R. "Professional Liability of Psychiatrists." *Defense Law Journal*, 1972, *21*, 122-167.

Bergin, A. E., and Lambert, M. J. "The Evaluation of Therapeutic Outcome." In A. E. Bergin and S. L. Garfield (Eds.), *Handbook of Psychotherapy and Behavior Change: An Empirical Analysis.* (2nd ed.) New York: Wiley, 1978.

Bernstein, B. E. "Malpractice: An Ogre on the Horizon." *Social Work*, 1978, *1*, 106-112.

Bersoff, D. N. "Therapists as Protectors and Policemen: New Roles as a Result of *Tarasoff.*" *Professional Psychology*, 1976, *6*, 267-273.

Brophy, J. J. "Suicide Attempts with Psychotherapeutic Drugs." *Archives of General Psychiatry*, 1967, *17*, 652-657.

Brownfain, J. J. "The APA Professional Liability Insurance Program." *American Psychologist*, 1971, *26*, 648-652.

Burns, R. E. "Psychotherapist-Patient Privilege, Patients' Dangerous Condition in Confidentiality, Legal Duty to Warn Potential Victim." *Akron Law Review*, 1975, *9* (1), 191-198.

Bursten, B. "Dimensions of Third Party Protection." *Bulletin of the American Academy of Law and Psychiatry*, 1978, *6* (4), 405-413.

Cassidy, P. S. "The Liability of Psychiatrists for Malpractice." *University of Pittsburgh Law Review*, 1974, *36*, 108-137.

"Cause of Action Can Be Stated Against Psychotherapists Employed by University Hospital and Against Campus Police, for Breach of Duty to Warn Victim of Peril from Patient as Disclosed by Patient's Communications." *Houston Law Review*, 1975, *12*, 968-988.

Cohen, R. J. *Malpractice: A Guide for Mental Health Professionals.* New York: Free Press, 1979.

Cohen, R. N. "*Tarasoff* v. *Regents of the University of California,* The Duty to Warn: Common Law and Statutory Problems for California Psychotherapists." *California Western Law Review*, 1978, *14*, 153-182.

Daley, D. W. "*Tarasoff* and the Psychotherapist's Duty to Warn." *San Diego Law Review*, 1975, *12*, 932-956.

Dawidoff, D. J. "Some Suggestions to Psychiatrists for Avoiding Legal Jeopardy." *Archives of General Psychiatry*, 1973a, *29*, 699-701.

Dawidoff, D. J. *The Malpractice of Psychiatrists: Malpractice in Psychoanalysis, Psychotherapy, and Psychiatry.* Springfield, Ill.: Thomas, 1973b.

Dawidoff, D. J. "Insanity, Intimacy, and Infidelity: Trends in Psychiatric Malpractice." *Trial*, 1977, *13* (6), 20-30.

DeLeon, P. H., and Borreliz, M. "Malpractice: Professional Liability and the Law." *Professional Psychology*, 1978, *8*, 467-477.

Dix, G. E. "*Tarasoff* and the Duty to Warn Potential Victims." In C. K. Hofling (Ed.), *Law and Ethics in the Practice of Psychiatry.* New York: Brunner/Mazel, 1981.

"Duty to Act for Protection of Another, Liability of Psychotherapist for Failure to Warn of Homicide Threatened by Patient." *Vanderbilt Law Review*, 1975, *28*, 631-639.

Eger, C. L. "Psychotherapists' Liability for Extrajudicial Breaches of Confidentiality." *Arizona Law Review*, 1976, *18*, 1061-1094.

Epstein, G. N., and others. "Panel Report: Impact of Law on Practice of Psychotherapy." *Journal of Law and Psychiatry*, 1977, *5*, 7-40.

Farberow, N. L., and Shneidman, E. S. *The Cry for Help.* New York: McGraw-Hill, 1961.

Feld, B. "The Psychiatrist's Liability for Malpractice." *Psychiatric Opinion*, 1971, *8*, 6-11.

Feldman, S. R., and Ward, T. W. "Psychotherapeutic Injury: Reshaping the Implied Contract as an Alternative to Malpractice." *North Carolina Law Review*, 1979, *58*, 63-96.

Fink, V. N. "Medical Malpractice: The Liability of Psychiatrists." *Notre Dame Lawyer*, 1973, *48*, 693-708.

Fishalow, S. E. "The Tort Liability of the Psychiatrist." *Bulletin of the American Academy of Law and Psychiatry*, 1975, *3*, 191-230.

Fleming, J. G., and Maximov, B. "The Patient or His Victim: The Therapist's Dilemma." *California Law Review,* 1974, *62,* 1025-1068.

Frank, T. D., and others. *Effective Ingredients of Successful Psychotherapy.* New York: Brunner/Mazel, 1978.

Freeman, L., and Roy, J. *Betrayal.* New York: Stein and Day, 1976.

Furrow, B. "Defective Mental Treatment: A Proposal for the Application of Strict Liability to Psychiatric Services." *Boston University Law Review,* 1978, *58,* 391-434.

Furrow, B. *Malpractice in Psychotherapy.* Lexington, Mass.: Lexington Books, 1980.

Garcetti, G., and Suarez, J. M. "The Liability of Psychiatric Hospitals for the Acts of Their Patients." *American Journal of Psychiatry,* 1968, *124,* 961-968.

Glassman, M. S. "Confidential Communications—Privileged Communications, Psychiatry—Psychotherapist Has a Duty to Warn an Endangered Victim Whose Peril Was Disclosed by Communications Between the Psychotherapist and Patient." *Cincinnati Law Review,* 1975, *44,* 368-375.

Glenn, R. D. "Standard of Care in Administering Non-Traditional Psychotherapy." *University of California, Davis Law Review,* 1974, *7,* 56-83.

Green, R. K., and Cox, G. "Social Work and Malpractice: A Converging Course." *Social Work,* 1978, *1,* 100-105.

Griffith, E. J., and Griffith, E. E. H. "Duty to Third Parties, Dangerousness and the Right to Refuse Treatment: Problematic Concepts for Psychiatrist and Lawyer." *California Western Law Review,* 1978, *14* (2), 241-274.

Grossman, M. "Right to Privacy vs. Right to Know." In W. E. Barton and C. J. Sanborn (Eds.), *Law and the Mental Health Professions: Friction at the Interface.* New York: International Universities Press, 1978.

Gurevitch, H. "*Tarasoff*: Protective Privilege Versus Public Peril." *American Journal of Psychiatry,* 1977, *134,* 289-292.

Haley, J. *Problem-Solving Therapy: New Strategies for Effective Family Therapy.* San Francisco: Jossey-Bass, 1976.

Halleck, S. L. *Law in the Practice of Psychiatry: A Handbook for Clinicians.* New York: Plenum, 1980.

Hamilton, J. M. "Malpractice from the Private Practice and Institutional Psychiatric Viewpoint." *Maryland State Medical Journal,* 1970, *1,* 69-74.

Harris, M. "Tort Liability of the Psychotherapist." *University of San Francisco Law Review,* 1973, *8,* 405-436.

Hofling, C. K. (Ed.). *Law and Ethics in the Practice of Psychiatry.* New York: Brunner/Mazel, 1981.

Hogan, D. B. *The Regulation of Psychotherapists.* Vol. 3: *A Review of Malpractice Suits in the United States.* Cambridge, Mass.: Ballinger, 1979.

Holmes, T. H., and Rahe, R. N. "The Social Readjustment Rating Scale." *Journal of Psychosomatic Research,* 1967, *11,* 213-218.

Howell, J. A. "Civil Liability for Suicide: An Analysis of the Causation Issue." *Arizona State Law Journal,* 1978, pp. 578-615.

Kaplan, R. B. "Psychotherapists, Policemen, and the Duty to Warn—An Unreasonable Extension of the Common Law." *Golden Gate University Law Review,* 1975, *6,* 229-248.

Kennedy, C. A. "Injuries Precipitated by Psychotherapy: Liability Without Fault as a Basis for Recovery." *South Dakota Law Review,* 1975, *20,* 401-417.

Kermani, E. "Psychotherapy: Legal Aspects." *Psychiatry Digest,* 1977, *38* (9), 33-39.

Knapp, S. "A Primer on Malpractice for Psychologists." *Professional Psychology,* 1980, *11* (4), 606-612.

Kozol, H. "The Diagnosis of Dangerousness." In S. Pasternak (Ed.), *Violence and Victims.* New York: Spectrum Publications, Halsted Press, 1975.

Krauskopf, J. M., and Krauskopf, C. J. "Torts and Psychologists." *Journal of Counseling Psychology,* 1965, *12* (3), 227-237.

Lane, P. J., and Spruill, J. "To Tell or Not to Tell: The Psychotherapist's Dilemma." *Psychotherapy: Theory, Research, and Practice,* 1980, *17* (2), 202-209.

Lebensohn, Z. "Defensive Psychiatry or How to Treat the Mentally Ill Without Being a Lawyer." In W. E. Barton and C. J. Sanborn (Eds.), *Law and the Mental Health Professions: Friction at the Interface.* New York: International Universities Press, 1978.

Lee, J. V. "A Psychotherapist Who Knows or Should Know His Patient Intends Violence to Another Incurs a Duty to Warn." *Cumberland Law Review,* 1977, *7,* 550-559.

Lee, V. "The Dangerous Patient Exception and the Duty to Warn: Creation of a Dangerous Precedent." *University of California, Davis Law Review,* 1976, *9,* 549-568.

Leonard, J. B. "A Therapist's Duty to Potential Victims: A Non-Threatening View of *Tarasoff.*" *Law and Human Behavior,* 1977, *1,* 309-317.

Leroy, D. H. "The Potential Criminal Liability of Human Sex Clinics and Their Patients." *St. Louis University Law Journal,* 1972, *16,* 586-603.

"Liability of Mental Hospitals for Acts of Those Patients Under the Open Door Policy." *Virginia Law Review,* 1971, *57,* 156-169.

Litman, R. E. "Medical-Legal Aspects of Suicide." *Washburn Law Journal,* 1967, *6,* 395-401.

Love, G. H., and Yanity, G. J. "Psychotherapy and the Law." *Medical Trial Technique Quarterly,* 1974, *20,* 405-429.

Lowe, R. H. "Risk Allocation in Mental Health Care: Whether to Treat the Patient or His Victim." *Utah Law Review,* 1975, 553-569.

Malcolm, J. J. "Duty Imposed upon Psychotherapists to Exercise Reasonable Care to Warn Potential Victims of Foreseeably Imminent Dangers Posed by Mentally Ill Patients." *Seton Hall Law Review,* 1975, *6,* 536-550.

Margulies, R. B. "Psychiatric Negligence." *Drake Law Review,* 1974, *23,* 640-652.

Martin, R. *Legal Challenges to Behavior Modification.* Champaign, Ill.: Research Press, 1975.

Mason, P. E., and Stitham, M. D. "The Expensive Dalliance: Assessing the Cost of Patient-Therapist Sex." *Bulletin of the American Academy of Law and Psychiatry,* 1977, *5,* 450-455.

Megargee, E. J. "The Prediction of Violence with Psychological Tests." In C. Spelberger (Ed.), *Current Topics in Clinical and Community Psychology*. New York: Academic Press, 1970.

Messinger, S. "Malpractice Suits—The Psychiatrist's Turn." *Journal of Legal Medicine*, 1975, *1*, 31-39.

Mirakian, S. "California Expansion of the Duty to Warn." *Washburn Law Journal*, 1976, *15*, 496-502.

Morrison, J., Frederick, M., and Rosenthal, H. J. "Contracting Confidentiality in Group Psychotherapy." *Forensic Psychology*, 1975, *7*, 4-5.

Morrow, K. "Psychotherapist Has a Duty to Warn an Endangered Victim Whose Peril Was Disclosed to Psychotherapist by Patient." *North Dakota Law Review*, 1976, *53*, 179-284.

Morse, H. N. "The Tort Liability of the Psychiatrist." *Syracuse Law Review*, 1967, *18*, 691-727.

Nesbit, N. A. "*Tarasoff* v. *Regents of the University of California*: Psychotherapists' Obligation of Confidentiality Versus the Duty to Warn." *Tulsa Law Journal*, 1977, *12*, 747-757.

Olander, A. J. "Discovery of Psychotherapist-Patient Communications After *Tarasoff*." *San Diego Law Review*, 1978, *15*, 265-285.

Oldham, J. T. "Liability of Therapists to Non-Patients." *Journal of Clinical Child Psychology*, 1978, *3*, 187-188.

Olsen, T. A. "Imposing a Duty to Warn on Psychiatrists—A Judicial Threat to the Psychiatric Profession." *University of Colorado Law Review*, 1977, *48*, 283-310.

Paul, R. E. "*Tarasoff* and the Duty to Warn: Toward a Standard of Conduct That Balances the Rights of Clients Against the Rights of Third Parties." *Professional Psychology*, 1977, *7*, 125-128.

Pendley, W. P. "The Dangerous Psychiatric Patient—The Doctor's Duty to Warn." *Land and Water Law Review*, 1975, *10*, 593-606.

Perr, I. N. "Suicide Responsibilities of Hospital and Psychiatrist." *Cleveland-Marshall Law Review*, 1960, *3* (9), 427-440.

Perr, I. N. "Legal Aspects of Sexual Therapies." *Journal of Legal Medicine*, 1975, *1*, 33-38.

Pollack, S. "Psychiatric-Legal Problems of Office Practice." *Current Psychiatric Therapies,* 1977, pp. 31-46.

Pope, K. S., Simpson, N. H., and Weiner, M. F. "Malpractice in Outpatient Psychotherapy." *American Journal of Psychotherapy,* 1978, *32* (4), 593-602.

Prosser, W. L. *Handbook of the Law of Torts.* St. Paul, Minn.: West, 1964.

"Psychiatrist Duty to the Public: Protection from Dangerous Patients." *Law Forum,* 1976, *4,* 1103-1128.

"Psychiatry and the Law: Duty to Warn Potential Victim of a Homicidal Patient." *New York Law School Law Review,* 1977, *22,* 1011-1022.

"Psychotherapists' Liability for the Release of Mentally Ill Offenders: A Proposed Expansion of the Theory of Strict Liability." *University of Pennsylvania Law Review,* 1977, *126,* 204-240.

Riskin, L. L. "Sexual Relations Between Psychotherapists and Their Patients: Toward Research or Restraint." *California Law Review,* 1979, *67,* 1000-1027.

Roby, J. J. "Getting Caught in the Open Door: Psychiatrists' Patients and Third Parties." *Mental Disability Law Reporter,* 1976, pp. 220-238.

Roston, R. A., and Sherrer, C. W. "Malpractice: What's New." *Professional Psychology,* 1973, *8,* 270-276.

Roth, L. H. "Clinical and Legal Considerations in the Therapy of Violence Prone Patients." *Current Psychiatric Therapies,* 1978, pp. 55-63.

Roth, L. H., and Meisel, A. "Dangerousness, Confidentiality and the Duty to Warn." *American Journal of Psychiatry,* 1977, *134,* 508-511.

Rothblatt, H. B., and Leroy, D. H. "Avoiding Psychiatric Malpractice." *California Western Law Review,* 1973, *9,* 260-272.

Rothenberg, K. H. "The Application of the *Tarasoff* Duty to Forensic Psychiatry." *Virginia Law Review,* 1980, *66* (3), 715-726.

Sauer, J. G. "Psychiatric Malpractice—A Survey." *Washburn Law Journal,* 1972, *11,* 461-470.

Saxe, D. B. "Psychotherapeutic Treatment and Malpractice." *Kentucky Law Journal,* 1970, *58,* 467-481.

Schindler, R. J. "Malpractice—Another New Dimension of Liability—A Critical Analysis." *Trial Lawyers Guide,* 1976, *20,* 129-151.

Schwartz, V. E. "Civil Liability for Causing Suicide: A Synthesis of Law and Psychiatry." *Vanderbilt Law Review,* 1971, *24,* 217-256.

Schwitzgebel, R. L., and Schwitzgebel, R. K. *Law and Psychological Practice.* New York: Wiley, 1980.

Seligman, B. S. "Untangling *Tarasoff: Tarasoff* v. *Regents of the University of California.*" *Hastings Law Journal,* 1977, *29,* 179-210.

Shaffer, T. L. "Undue Influence, Confidential Relationship and the Psychology of Transference." *Notre Dame Lawyer,* 1969, *45,* 197-237.

Shea, T. E. "Legal Standards of Care for Psychiatrists and Psychologists." *Western State University Law Review,* 1979, *6,* 79-99.

Slaby, A. E., Lieb, J., and Tancredi, L. P. *Handbook of Psychiatric Emergencies.* Flushing, N.Y.: Medical Examination Publishing Co., 1975.

Slawson, P. F. "Psychiatric Malpractice: A Regional Incidence Study." *American Journal of Psychiatry,* 1970, *126,* 1302-1305.

Slawson, P. F. "Psychiatric Malpractice: The California Experience." *American Journal of Psychiatry,* 1979, *136* (5), 650-654.

Slawson, P. F., Flinn, D. E., and Schwartz, D. A. "Legal Responsibility for Suicide." *Psychiatric Quarterly,* 1974, *48,* 50-64.

Sloan, J. B., and Klein, S. B. "Psychotherapeutic Disclosures: A Conflict Between Right and Duty." *Toledo Law Review,* 1977, *9,* 57-72.

Slovenko, R. "The Impact of the Law on Psychiatric Practice." *Career Directions,* 1976, *5,* 33-34.

Slovenko, R. "On the Legal Aspects of Tardive Dyskinesia." *Journal of Law and Psychiatry,* 1979, *7* (3), 295-331.

Slovenko, R. "Legal Issues in Psychotherapy Supervision." In A. K. Hess (Ed.), *Psychotherapy Supervision: Theory, Research, Practice.* New York: Wiley, 1980.

Stone, A. A. "Suicide Precipitated by Psychotherapy: A Clinical Contribution." *American Journal of Psychotherapy,* 1971, *25,* 18-21.

Stone, A. A. "The Legal Implications of Sexual Activity Between Psychiatrist and Patient." *American Journal of Psychiatry,* 1976a, *133* (10), 1138-1141.

Stone, A. A. "The *Tarasoff* Decision: Suing Psychotherapists to Safeguard Society." *Harvard Law Review,* 1976b, *90,* 358-378.

Strupp, H., Hadley, S. W., and Gomes-Schwartz, B. *Psychotherapy for Better or Worse.* New York: Aronson, 1977.

Tabachnick, N. D., and Farberow, N. L. "The Assessment of Self-Destructive Potentiality." In N. L. Farberow and E. S. Schneidman (Eds.), *The Cry for Help.* New York: McGraw-Hill, 1961.

Tancredi, L., Lieb, J., and Slaby, A. *Legal Issues in Psychiatric Care.* New York: Harper & Row, 1975.

Tarshis, C. B. "Liability for Psychotherapy." *Toronto University Faculty of Law Review,* 1972, *30,* 75-96.

Trent, C. L. "Psychiatric Malpractice Insurance and Its Problems: An Overview." In W. E. Barton and C. J. Sanborn (Eds.), *Law and the Mental Health Professions: Friction at the Interface.* New York: International Universities Press, 1978.

Trent, C. L., and Muhl, W. P. "Professional Liability Insurance and the American Psychiatrist." *American Journal of Psychiatry,* 1975, *132,* 1312-1314.

Tryon, W. W. "Behavior Modification Therapy and the Law." *Professional Psychology,* 1976, *6,* 468-474.

Twardy, S. "The Issue of Malpractice in Psychiatry." *Medical Trial Techniques Quarterly,* 1978, *25,* 161-176.

Valentine, G. H. "*Tarasoff* v. *Regents of University of California:* The Psychotherapist's Peril." *University of Pittsburgh Law Review,* 1975, *37,* 155-162.

Van Hoose, W. H., and Kottler, J. A. *Ethical and Legal Issues in Counseling and Psychotherapy.* San Francisco: Jossey-Bass, 1977.

Waltzer, H. "Malpractice Liability in a Patient's Suicide." *American Journal of Psychotherapy,* 1980, *34* (1), 89-98.

Wexler, D. B. "Patients, Therapists, and Third Parties: The Victimological Virtues of *Tarasoff*." *International Journal of Law and Psychiatry*, 1979, *2*, 1-28.

White, A. E., and Gross, R. B. "Professional Liability Insurance and the Psychologist." *Professional Psychology*, 1975, *8*, 267-273.

Wigmore, J. H. *Evidence.* Boston: Little, Brown, 1961.

Wise, T. P. "Where the Public Peril Begins: A Survey of Psychotherapists to Determine the Effects of *Tarasoff*." *Stanford Law Review*, 1978, *31*, 165-190.

Index

196